Loss, Grief and Existential Awareness

Loss, Grief and Existential Awareness introduces the integrated process model (IPM), a new interdisciplinary and interprofessional model for grief research, education, and accompaniment that distinguishes and integrates five dimensions of grief: physical, emotional, cognitive, social, and spiritual.

Central in this book is the insight that grief is connected to love because it is rooted in losing what is meaningful and dear to us. Once we recognize this, grief can become a window to existential awareness. Combining research on the physical, emotional, cognitive, social, and spiritual dimensions of grief, the integrated process approach connects this quest for a personal and authentic answer to the big questions in life with the philosophical and therapeutic tradition of existential thinking. Structured in an accessible, informative manner with gradual information building, the book presents the IPM approach at the beginning and then turns to it as a model throughout the book, so the reader gradually will start to deepen their understanding and memorize the framework. The structure is enhanced with boxes with existential reflections and exercises to engage the reader and case presentations of grieving persons who are followed throughout the book.

This book is meant for everyone who is interested in a deeper understanding of how loss and grief can help open the door to a more meaningful way of living. It is especially helpful for healthcare professionals, therapists, counsellors, chaplains, and researchers.

Mai-Britt Guldin is an authorized psychologist, certified specialist in psychotherapy and supervision, Ph.D., from the Institute for Public Health, Aarhus University, Denmark. She is former professor and research director. Now, she works as senior researcher and director at the Center for Grief and Existential Values.

Carlo Leget is currently full professor in care ethics at the University of Humanistic Studies in Utrecht, the Netherlands, and working at the Center for Grief and Existential Values.

Loss, Grief and Existential Awareness

An Integrative Approach

Mai-Britt Guldin and Carlo Leget

Routledge
Taylor & Francis Group

LONDON AND NEW YORK

Designed cover image: Tuscany sunset landscape view of green hills ringed with cypress trees. Italy, Europe. © Getty Images 1212781992

First published in 2025
by Routledge
4 Park Square, Milton Park, Abingdon, Oxon OX14 4RN

and by Routledge
605 Third Avenue, New York, NY 10158

Routledge is an imprint of the Taylor & Francis Group, an informa business

British Library Cataloguing-in-Publication Data
A catalogue record for this book is available from the British Library

Library of Congress Cataloging-in-Publication Data
Names: Guldin, Mai-Britt, author. | Leget, Carlo, author.
Title: Loss, grief and existential awareness : an integrative approach / Mai-Britt Guldin and Carlo Leget.
Description: Abingdon, Oxon ; New York, NY : Routledge, 2025. | Includes bibliographical references and index.
Identifiers: LCCN 2024032387 (print) | LCCN 2024032388 (ebook) | ISBN 9781032812847 (hardback) | ISBN 9781032812786 (paperback) | ISBN 9781003499060 (ebook)
Subjects: LCSH: Grief. | Loss (Psychology)
Classification: LCC BF575.G7 G8495 2025 (print) | LCC BF575.G7 (ebook) | DDC 155.9/37—dc23/eng/20240918
LC record available at https://lccn.loc.gov/2024032387
LC ebook record available at https://lccn.loc.gov/2024032388

ISBN: 978-1-032-81284-7 (hbk)
ISBN: 978-1-032-81278-6 (pbk)
ISBN: 978-1-003-49906-0 (ebk)

DOI: 10.4324/9781003499060

Typeset in Times New Roman
by Apex CoVantage, LLC

Contents

Preface

Mai-Britt Guldin: It has been quite a few years since I started my work with grief as a psychologist and specialist in psychotherapy and later wrote a Ph.D. about how grief is treated in the healthcare system. I have spoken to hundreds of grieving people over the years, and my experience is that as we grieve, we are invited to look at ourselves, our lives, and to make changes. For me, working with loss and grief has always inspired contemplation, devotion, longing, gentleness, humility, and increased love. Grief has become a prism through which I look at the world. I think grief deepens my understanding of love and life and especially lends clarity to love and my values. At the same time, grief is an intense, dramatic, violent force that puts us in contact with death, destruction, transcendence, and eternity. Many mourners tell me that they live with death and destruction close at hand. This makes loss and grief open to fundamental existential considerations about meaning, purpose, loneliness, powerlessness, and taking responsibility for one's own life. While working on my research projects and writing books, I struggled to understand the depth of grief, its poetic side, and even its raw beauty. It was as if there was one type of logic in the research on grief and grief support and a completely different type of logic in my psychotherapeutic work with grieving people, in the great novels about grief, in the philosophy of existence and beautiful poems about loss. My clients time and again introduced existential questions into the sessions, or they brought poems or literature that resonated with their suffering. This made so much sense to me, and I struggled to make the research meet the lived experience. Although my study of existentialism or collecting novels and essays about grief can mostly be called a autodidact education, it helped me feel at home in both grief research and grief therapy. I would not have developed the passion for grief research without it. I often had the feeling that it was difficult to make my many ways of thinking about the subject fit together in a unified understanding of grief. It was only when I met Carlo that my different ways of thinking or experiencing the field began to converge and develop into a greater whole.

Carlo Leget: Since my education in theology and my Ph.D. on life and death in the theology of Thomas Aquinas, I have been fascinated by the transformative potential of the spiritual and existential. Life is movement and development, and being alive as a human means for most of us to become aware of this. As we grow older, we find that our outlook on life changes, and we become aware that we are mortal. Paradoxically, it is loss and suffering that play an important role in our maturation as humans. Although confronting the dark and heavy side of life is never a guarantee of transforming into a more mature person, there is a mysterious relationship between adversity and growth. In my academic work, I have studied meaning and spirituality at the end of life for many years, predominantly from a philosophical and spiritual perspective. When my conversations with Mai-Britt started a few years ago, I discovered a mind full of compassion and with an education that was completely complementary. I began to realize that the activity of the human mind, where we are constantly searching for meaning, is not something only philosophy deals with. Searching for meaning is an activity subject to human consciousness, which is central to psychology as well. Mai-Britt invited me to reconsider many of the views I had developed up to that point, and this process underlies the ideas in this book.

We have worked together on the book, the Integrative Process Model of loss and grief, and the understanding of existential growth through loss and grief over a period of almost two years. The book brings together our backgrounds in spiritual care, care ethics, psychology, and palliative care. In this process, the ideas leapt out at us for each model draft we drew and for each page we wrote. The creativity seemed enormous, and the joy of working together has been and continues to be very inspiring. In this process, we started the Center for Grief and Existential Values and published an article in *Death Studies* (Guldin & Leget, 2023) in which we laid the scientific foundation for this book.

We work both from our office a stone's throw from Aarhus Cathedral, an impressive Romanesque basilica in Gothic style in the middle of Aarhus, Denmark, and a beautiful and sunny apartment among the treetops in Zeist, close to Utrecht in the Netherlands. Many of our thoughts have been developed in conversation while enjoying our cottage by the water, going on nature retreats, hiking, and writing. Although this book is the fruit of 20 years of work in academia and in clinical work, it is not the end of a project. It is the beginning of a process in which we seek to establish a new understanding of loss and grief around its existential dimension. Our intention is to open the understanding of the many disciplines and professions that have worked on and with the phenomenon of grief for decades. We hope to engage the reader in this process and begin a journey toward a better understanding of the meaning of loss and grief and its transformative potential in our lives.

Aarhus and Zeist, Spring 2024,
Mai-Britt Guldin & Carlo Leget

Chapter 1

Loss as the ultimate limitation of human existence

Come, grief.
Show me the meaning of my loss.
Let me honor you.

Text box 1.1   The old man lost his horse

Once upon a time, there was a righteous man who lived near the border. One day one of his horses broke loose and ran into barbarian territory. All his neighbors felt sorry for him, but his father said, "Who knows what it will bring?" After a few months the horse came back and brought a group of good barbarian horses with him. Everyone congratulated the man, but his father said, "Who knows what it will bring?" When the man's son was riding one of the horses, he fell off and broke a leg. All the neighbors felt sorry for him, but the father said, "Who knows what it will bring?" A year later the barbarians invaded the country and all men had to join the army to defend the country. The son, who had broken his leg, was exempted and allowed to stay at home. In the battle that followed, nine out of ten frontiersmen were killed, but both father and son survived.

(Wikipedia)

This Chinese parable, which is more than 2,000 years old, has been interpreted in many ways. At first glance, this story is about a series of accidents. What struck us about this story is that it is very much about loss and events that no one would seek voluntarily. At the same time, the story invites us to understand the ambiguity of both loss and gain. Perhaps we are even invited to embrace a broader understanding of how to make sense of our losses.

DOI: 10.4324/9781003499060-1

> Loss and change are painful,
> but we can't change the pain
> before we have accepted it
> and made a choice about what we want to do with it.

In short, the parable opens our eyes to the fact that what appears to be a heartbreaking loss at first glance has the potential over time to open up possibilities we could never have dreamed of. It may even possess the power of an existential change in life.

This book invites you to a new understanding of loss and grief. It asks you to let go of many preconceived notions, opinions, and ideas. We invite you to look at loss and grief with open or even fresh eyes and look at the full spectrum of reactions that come with it. We are not trying to convince you that loss is pleasant or that something good comes with every loss. If you've ever experienced loss, we probably couldn't convince you of this anyway. You will most likely already know that loss and grief are painful and can be heartbreaking and full of suffering. You will also know that if given the opportunity, we would all like to avoid the loss, grief, and suffering, but most often, we do not possess the power to prevent the losses we experience. No matter how untimely, unfair, or destructive they may seem, in this book, we consider them an inevitable part of life. With loss and grief, it follows that we must naturally look at our life and the way we live it and reflect on what is important to us and what the meaning of what we experience is. For most people, this will mean an increased existential awareness. But even with a very painful loss, there is no guarantee that a strengthened existential consciousness will arise from it. But we will point to many reasons this can happen.

Loss and grief are among life's most decisive and defining experiences. We see this when grief is a central theme in studies of culture and cultural rituals about death and the dying, funerals, and memorial rituals (Silverman et al., 2021). Many of the world's literary traditions, from the Epic of Gilgamesh to Shakespeare's characters, suffer from grief; countless songs and poems depict the pain of grief; movies, podcasts, and countless personal memoirs revolve around the theme of loss and grief. We just need to ask one person who is grieving. There can be no doubt that loss and grief are inevitable parts of human life. We live and die and we love and lose. Therefore, loss and grief are part of every human life, intrinsic existential experiences for all of us. We struggle with our losses, and when we lose something that is most precious to us, the losses stand to us as the ultimate limitation of our human existence.

Loss is considered the ultimate limitation to human existence.

We have become accustomed to the fact that when we talk about loss in life, it is about another person dying. Loss can be about the bonds with our loved ones, and we are probably used to thinking about loss and grief in connection with love relationships. However, a life with a lot of love is not the same as a life without loss and sorrow, since everything we care about and that is important to us ends in loss. Even when we have lost a loved one, we do not stop loving them, and therefore, this love can even be said to be subject to continued loss. For the rest of our lives, we may be reminded of what we no longer have. This led the well-known grief researcher Colin Murray Parkes to say that grief is always a form of love and the price we pay for love. Therefore, this book is as much about love and gratitude as it is about loss and grief.

But our love is not just about other people. The most common understanding of loss and grief is that it is about losing a close person to death and going through a grieving process. But not all losses have to do with death. The experience of loss and the response grief has to do with all our connections to the world, everything that matters to us, which you might call a love of many different aspects of life. So take a moment to consider:

What situations other than death give you the experience of loss?

You will discover that loss and grief are not only processes associated with limited events, such as losing a loved one to illness and death, but that we encounter loss on a regular basis in connection with many different types of significant life-changing events.

We love and connect with the world, our culture, and time, and we are always working on connectedness to ourselves, our past, and our future. These connections are also subject to losses.

Everything that is meaningful to us
and with which we connect or find meaning
can be lost.
We grieve for it all.

Studies show that grief over losses other than death also plays a significant role for us and especially losses that have to do with a role that we have played in our lives, such as losing a job or divorce (Papa et al., 2014). In fact, many life-changing events can spur our sense of loss, and in one study, college students reported that losses such as the bereavement of a boyfriend or a broken engagement played a much more significant role than losses resulting from death (Varga, 2016). Many parents will tell you that their greatest sense of loss is connected to their greatest love, namely their children. There is a feeling of great love but also great loss if our child is handicapped, becomes ill, or does not function as expected or when they suffer in their mental or social life. Loss and grief can be associated with death in relation to a specific person but also death in a more abstract sense: namely the unlived. Therefore, we write this book with the basic understanding that:

> We can lose everything that connects us to the world or ourselves,
> everything that constitutes our being in the world
> and defines our identity and vitality.
> We grieve for it all. Also what is unlived in our lives.

This makes loss and grief one of the most common experiences in human existence, and we encounter it many times in life. The complex context we experience in life, the connections to our loved ones, every relationship, everyday experiences, abilities, functions, status, roles, resources, opportunities, ambitions, dreams, values, ideals, and much more, make up our being in the world and our meaning in life and thus our vitality. All of that can be lost, leaving us with an overwhelming sense of hurt, sadness, despair, grief, deprivation, emptiness, and meaninglessness. After a significant loss, the world is forever changed. In the turbulence or vacuum that occurs after a loss, it is common to feel disillusioned, disoriented, and out of touch with life. For a while, nothing makes sense anymore.

> A space opens up that requires us to hold in our hands
> life's most important paradox:
> The life we have been given and all the connections we have made
> —we will surely lose it all again.

This means that every time we love or find meaning in something, we are confronted with the basic fact of life, that we will lose it again, and our loved ones will one day lose us. When we love, there is usually a fear of losing it again. In this perspective, loss is as fundamental to human life as love.

But loss is not only a limitation. Viktor Frankl (1905–1997), one of the first psychiatrists to deal with human existence in his therapeutic method, called loss and grief fundamental existential experiences. He also described that loss and grief are absolutely primary in creating movement in our lives:

> When we experience loss, we are pushed into a tension
> "between what one has already achieved and what one still ought to accomplish,
> or the gap between what one is and what one should become."
>
> (Frankl, 1946/2006)

The gap between what we want in life and what we have lost creates a tension or a space where we must now make changes and look for meaning. This gives us a basic existential tension or suffering.

All losses bring us existential suffering,
and all existential suffering involves loss and grief.
Every loss makes us think about our life and what is the meaning of it.
Therefore, loss and grief are at the core of existential suffering.

What this book is about

This book is about how we can create a more holistic understanding of loss and grief. It is written with the purpose of understanding loss and grief as essential existential experiences in human life that we all face many times throughout life and struggle with as we try to stay connected to ourselves, our present, past, and future.

As the book unfolds a holistic understanding of loss and grief, it will become clear that it builds on a large number of writers and artists who have worked on this subject. Not least, it builds on the work that has been developed in recent decades by researchers from various professional disciplines.

Loss and grief are very painful parts of life. A loss of a parent, a spouse, a child, a job, a body part, a lifelong dream—these are all unique, intense, and overwhelming turning points in an individual's life. Often, it gives a vulnerability in life, and the experience will now shape the person's life and future. In this struggle, it is easy to believe that the loss we suffered is more painful than the losses of others, that we are unique because of this particular loss, or that no one understands our suffering. Then, we isolate ourselves and fail to see the universality of loss and the basic existential suffering of all individuals. There can be no doubt that, for example, losing a parent in childhood is a life-changing experience that increases vulnerability and defines the young person and their future. But the danger is that we fail to recognize that another young person is also vulnerable due to other types of loss: parental divorce, mental illness in the family, emigration and a different ethnic background than the majority, sexual orientation, or family secrets that cause shame and many other problems. And are not all these incidents losses?

If we fail to see all of life's losses, there is a danger that we will not show sufficient sensitivity to our own losses and the losses of others, and ultimately, we will fail to recognize our shared experiences of the losses in human life. It means that we acknowledge our humanity, frailty, and the universality of human vulnerability. We begin to cry out for attention to the particular loss we have suffered, thinking that this will help, but we forget to see what connects us as human beings. Life is always a movement between love and loss, gratitude and sorrow, sensibility and suffering. This leaves room for another fundamental understanding in this book:

> It is clear that the experience of loss and grief
> is a widespread, natural, and common existential experience.
> That is why we as humans are united in loss and grief.

Acknowledging that we share the existential experience of loss and grief can quite fundamentally open us up to acknowledging the losses that other people suffer and respecting precisely their reactions to it. Mark Twain (1898/1967) once wrote that there is no objective measure for the grief that people feel: how could we ever compare the sorrow of a child losing a doll to a king losing a crown? The meaning of a loss is deeply personal, and respect for that meaning is linked to respect for the other person. Therefore, another fundamental understanding in this book is that:

> Only the griever can tell us,
> what is lost and what their grief is about
> —and how much grief is appropriate for them.

Grief is as much a fundamental part of being human and developing as a human being as love is. If we lose a loved one, that particular person and what they mean in our lives can never be replaced. The person was unique, and the bond between us is characteristic of our relationship. We are used to not questioning why another person loves the person they love, but we are not used to showing grief the same consideration and space. Yet if we deny the other person's love or grief, we deny their identity and perhaps ultimately our shared humanity. This idea is at the heart of this book. We grieve whenever we feel the loss of something beloved, heartfelt, meaningful, or valuable.

> Only the person can tell us,
> when they experience a loss
> and what this loss means to them.
> Grief must always be seen in this picture.
> For the individual, it is important to honor and express their grief,
> since the obligation for the person to show the significance of the loss to
>   the world
> is nonnegotiable.

Expressing and honoring our grief can be seen as an expression of the very essence of our being. Therefore, grief itself ultimately cannot be removed, treated, or cured by anyone. Any attempt to remove grief will only mean that the grieving person feels that we do not respect and honor the person or the loss or the love it expresses. Rather, it will probably be experienced as disrespectful, overstepping, and misunderstood. In this book, we are therefore concerned with how we become better at supporting each other in acknowledging our loss and expressing our grief as a central aspect of our existence.

In this perspective, grief is supreme and untouchable, as it is closely tied to the love and meaning each of us finds in life.

> Basically, grief is an expression of the self.
> It is a necessary self-expression so I can become even more myself.

An integrative grief model

Many books have been written about loss and grief. However, none of these have integrated different disciplines and professions and looked at grief as a fundamental existential experience with a power that can change our understanding of our lives. That is what this book aims for. It brings out another fundamental understanding in the book:

> The awareness of all the different losses in our lives
> can help us connect with ourselves
> and find a deeper understanding of our existence.

Therefore, in this book, we present a new, holistic and integrative model for loss and grief: the Integrative Process Model for Loss and Grief (IPM). The IPM aims to offer an interprofessional framework for professionals from different disciplines to foster an increased awareness of the phenomenon of grief. The framework can be used to understand grief, as it builds on existing research from different disciplines and at the same time provides key orientation points or stepping stones to provide support to each other or to oneself. This means that the model also offers opportunities for professional support, advice, and therapy.

Text box 1.2   The Integrative Process Model for loss and grief aims to

- offer an approach with a more nuanced understanding of the phenomenon of grief
- embrace the many different aspects of grief

- increase awareness of loss and grief as existential experiences
- better reflect and respect the individual's experience of loss
- create better understanding and care for the suffering we all experience through loss.

The basic understanding in the IPM is that loss is an existential condition. Therefore, this book presents how loss and grief introduce fundamental existential questions into life and ask us to answer them. Existential questions we all know, such as *Why is this happening to me? What should I do with it? What have I lost? How can I live with this loss? How can I believe in life again?* Loss and grief confront us with what we have no control over and thus our limitations. Loss also invites us to create change where there is an emptiness or a deficiency. In the book *Kafka on the Shore*, author Haruki Murakami (2002/2006) uses the image of finding yourself in a storm. The storm is beyond our control, and we cannot step out of it or make it stop. But this is exactly what the storm is about because when the storm is over, the experience will most likely have changed us in such a manner that we will not be the same person as before the storm. This is precisely what IPM also deals with. It points to a more comprehensive understanding of loss and grief and the role that both play in a life course, because grief is not only painful but also a force that can help us into a deeper understanding of ourselves and life. Therefore, the IPM presents loss as a potential for existential awareness that can help us live life more authentically.

There is no end to grief because there is no end to love.
Instead, loss invites us into a deeper existential awareness,
where we can become better connected with ourselves,
and from here, we can learn to live with our loss.

The ambiguity of loss

This book is concerned with what we call an integrative understanding of grief. The book is based on scientific studies and the various professional disciplines as well as great thinkers who have dealt with loss and grief. Nevertheless, it is important to point out that loss is a natural and fundamental part of life, and in order for us to live with our loss and to work on the awareness of the influence of loss on our life, an individual existential process takes place. We all have different reactions to loss, but the one thing we can be sure of is the emptiness, despair, and suffering that comes with our loss. When loss and grief are such a fundamental part of life, it also means that the loss has the potential to open up life's big existential questions about death and meaninglessness, which present themselves in the grieving process. It is basically about how all our losses and sorrows confront us with life's big questions and ambiguities.

Text box 1.3   The ambiguity of loss

- We are aware and consider why we must experience loss and grief, but the questions can only be answered through our own reflections.
- We have a free will and the ability to make choices about our reactions, but we can only take responsibility within the limits that life has imposed on us.
- We want to feel connected to ourselves, others, or life, but we have to face our existential conditions alone.
- We search for meaning in our experiences and in our life, but we never finish this search because it transcends ourselves and our own life.

An integrative approach to grief aims to enable each person to find their own balance in these existential paradoxes in life.

An integrative approach to grief
is not about providing the answers to how we can grieve.
It is about the essential understanding
that grief opens up a space for life's big questions.
There are no definitive answers here
but more or less authentic ways of dealing
with one's own existence.

Grief places demands on us. Loss and grief can be understood as a gateway that unlocks the existential questions and paradoxes for us but at the same time can lead us to a deeper understanding of our existence. Grief is filled with emptiness, despair, and suffering, but in this void, it also forces us to look up from the immediate suffering to take in what we have lost and what it means to us. In this process, we are adjusting to the loss and making decisions about the changed life and new future. This means that grief possesses a kind of power to lift our outlook on life, ask basic existential questions, and initiate the search for new meaning. This development gives loss and grief what might be called a transformative potential.

Grief asks us: What comes after your loss?

Here, the loss becomes not only an end but also a new beginning. A potential to change our entire understanding of life and our existence and possibly even the potential to develop as a person. Not because we want to or choose to, because this process is often painful and filled with more suffering when we cannot change the loss, but because we have to. In the meantime, we can end up fearing the grief and trying to avoid it or run away from it. However, this means that we do not see the whole process of grief and what it offers us. We fail to talk about what grief teaches us, and we risk missing out on embracing its powerful potential.

> Now that you have lost this significant part of your life,
> where are you going as a human being?

Loss and grief as access to existential awareness

Most theories and models of grief overlook the existential dimension. What is meant by the word *existential* in this regard? The word *existential* refers to a tradition of thought in European and North American culture that has developed over the past 200 years into a tree with many branches. Originally, the tradition goes back to the works of Søren Kierkegaard (1813–1855) and novelists such as Fyodor Dostoevsky (1821–1881). They inspired thinking about existence in the philosophical tradition that was later, in the 1940s and 1950s, called existentialism based on philosophers such as Martin Heidegger (1889–1976), Jean-Paul Sartre (1905–1980), and Albert Camus (1913–1960). Existential therapy arose from this via authors such as Viktor Frankl (1905–1997), Rollo May (1909–1994), Irvin D. Yalom (1931–), Ernesto Spinelli (1949–), and Emmy Van Deurzen (1951–).

Existentialist thinking is difficult to delineate and define, but there are a number of common interests and understandings that are useful for recognizing existentialist thinking (Craig, 2008). Existentialist thinkers are fundamentally interested in the question: What does it mean to be human? Or, put differently: How does human existence contrast with existing as a tree, a frog, or a buffalo? In this tradition of thought, the answer to this question can only be given by those who share this form of existence. There is no external authority, institution, or religion that can answer this fundamental question. And what is more: the answer to what it is like to exist as a human being is always a personal answer that can only be given by oneself. This is what existentialists claim life is all about:

> I formulate my personal answer to the great question of my existence
> and thereby find my own authenticity.

Living with authenticity is discussed by existentialists such as Heidegger, Sartre, Spinelli, and Yalom and means:

> To develop my freedom as a moral being
> and take responsibility for my life
> in order for me to live in accordance with my values.

The opposite of an authentic life is a life defined by others: the people around me, the expectations of my culture or a religion or an authority. According to traditional existentialist thinking, the lack of authenticity will cause existential anxiety such as worries about what is expected from me, whether I will get enough out of life, and anxiety about all the choices I have to make.

According to the existentialist tradition, the pursuit of an authentic life is not easy. According to Spinelli (2015) and Yalom (1980), we face several big central questions about life, which in their tradition are called the ultimate concerns of life and pertain to death, freedom, aloneness, and meaning.

Text box 1.4   Life's ultimate concerns

- The realization that we are mortal and will die ourselves one day
- The question of what I do with my basic freedom as a human being
- The fear of being alone and isolated from the rest of humanity
- The search for a meaningful life.

The ultimate concerns, these big and fundamental questions, define our humanity, and it takes courage to deal with them. Yalom (1980) and Spinelli (2015) point out that we all need to find an answer to these questions in order to live up to our full potential as human beings. It is easy to avoid the big questions by being preoccupied with all kinds of distractions that our society has to offer. Existentialist thinkers argue that this strategy may work for a while, but in the long run, it will prevent us from living a meaningful life. In order for life to be meaningful, we also have to deal with the difficult aspects of our existence that are related to suffering caused by, for example, loss, anxiety, meaninglessness, and isolation. They affect us all, and if we understand loss and grief out of context and perspective, we can easily come to believe that we are the only person in the world who is affected or suffers so much. If we do not deal with these aspects of life, then it will create even more anxiety and suffering when we lose or are faced with death or loneliness or big choices.

This is precisely why the IPM focuses on the existential dimension of loss and grief. The model therefore aims both to show that loss and grief are central to existential suffering and to show how loss and grief can lead us on the way to making choices, taking responsibility, and finding our own values and meaning in life. Loss and grief help us toward our authenticity.

Living the questions in the paradoxes of loss

As we move through our lives, we all find ourselves having to face the fundamental themes of human existence of death, freedom, loneliness, and meaning (Yalom, 1980). Yalom would say that even if we do not focus on it, we always live our lives in the shadow of these ultimate concerns or big questions of life. They are the root of our anxiety and restlessness in life. Perhaps we are not aware of the existential concerns until we have lost something or experienced great changes. Until then, we balance our existential anxiety in an inconspicuous or even unconscious way without necessarily encountering problems. But the second we experience loss, the existential concerns present themselves to us because we are shaken to the core of our existence. Now, existential themes and questions become the new norm.

Text box 1.5   When we experience loss, we ask ourselves

- Why is this happening to me?
- Do I deserve this?
- What is the meaning of my loss?
- How do I deal with death?
- What do I do about feeling alone?
- How can I continue my life?

Already 200 years ago, Kierkegaard (1849/1941) helped us to understand how human existence is full of paradoxes. A paradox is something that appears to be contradictory but makes complete sense in relation to our human experience. For example, we have free will, and at the same time, we are determined by our genes, upbringing, culture etc. As long as we live our daily life and we are busy with all the things that occupy us, we might not think much about these paradoxes. But as soon as our existence is shattered by a great loss, it is as if the paradoxes come to the surface. Great losses are like existential earthquakes: they make visible what is hidden and covered in normal life. Although these questions were there before the loss, the grieving process now makes them very present and more urgent. Perhaps especially because we are now constantly reminded of death or the finality of things.

The IPM points out that grief invites us into an opening, where the fundamental existential paradoxes present themselves before us as big questions in life, to which there seems to be no definite right answer. Some of the basic existential paradoxes we are confronted with in grief are described in the IPM.

Text box 1.6   Basic existential paradoxes in the IPM

- Only by dealing with death can we live life to the fullest.
- Only by accepting our feelings can we take responsibility for them.
- Only by feeling our loss can we understand our loss.
- Only by daring to be alone can we achieve connectedness.
- Only by experiencing meaninglessness can we discover meaning.

If we look at the existential paradoxes of loss, it quickly becomes clear that there are no clear or definite answers to the questions we ask ourselves.

> Some questions in life can be answered by experts.
> The question "What is the meaning of my loss?"
> cannot be answered by anyone but the questioner.

Here, it also applies that the answer cannot be found in an instant. Maybe this can be compared to the phenomenon that if you answer someone else's question, you pass on your knowledge to them. But if you instead ask them a good question, you teach them to find their own answers.

In his "Letter to a Young Poet," the German poet Rainer Maria Rilke (1875–1926) also points to this profound awareness. His advice is to be patient toward the big unresolved questions we carry with us in our lives. Looking actively for answers will not help us, because answers to life's big questions can only work if we are able to live them. Therefore, Rilke proposes to love the questions and live them. Only then we might someday discover that the questions have resolved and we notice that we live our way into the answer (Rilke, 1929/2000).

Maybe that is how it is with loss? Living with a great loss opens up a space with great existential questions. This space is defined by a fundamental tension we face while grieving: on the one hand, we constantly think about death, on the other hand, we have to live our lives. A significant value in life was taken from us, and the meaning of life has been temporarily dissolved. Perhaps we even feel that we want to join a loved one in death. Now, a space has been opened in which the tension between life and death is pushed to the forefront. We find ourselves in a new place in life where we ask ourselves big questions. The idea of this book is therefore also that it offers a wide range of existential reflections on loss and grief, thereby inviting the reader to reflect, to help us answer our own big questions.

If we are not getting through grief, then how to understand the process?

It is a popular understanding that grief is a process that we have to go through, and when we have readjusted life to the loss, it comes to an end. In the integrative understanding of grief, we argue that there is no end to grief. There is no end to love, and there is no solution to the great existential questions of life and death that arise in the grieving process. Therefore, grief will continue to appear even when it is integrated into our lives. Our connectedness to the lost will, in a way, make the grief eternally relevant, because we will always seek to honor the lost and express what it means to us. Instead, the integrative approach to grief works from the understanding that we seek a balance in the existential questions in our search for authenticity and meaning in life, and in this, we can find a meaningful expression of our grief.

An integrative approach to grief means that every person is invited into the ambiguity of the grief process and thus into the opening to life's fundamental existential questions. Now, grief gives us an opportunity to find a new balance in them.

In the integrative understanding, the only relief in the existential suffering
   of grief
is to acknowledge the loss, express and honor the grief,
and seek connection to ourselves, the lost, and the others, but also to the
   future.

Grief is expressed with our whole body and nervous system. It activates turmoil and anxiety but thereby also opens up contact with ourselves, our life history, and our previous situations of loss. This means that grief even invites us back in to look at old open-ended existential questions. This is both a challenge and an invitation, and we can accept it or reject it.

It is understandable that the suffering of our loss blinds us to the existential questions, because the pain can be overwhelming. The idea of the IPM is not to dismiss this pain, just as no one can promise that any kind of existential suffering will ultimately lead to more meaning, maturity, or vitality. Rather, the idea is to try to understand that only by facing the existential aspects of grief can we learn to live with loss.

The IPM proposes an approach to loss and grief,
where we can learn to live authentically with our loss
through openness, awareness, contact, connectedness, and existential
   reflection.

Here, the powerful transformative forces of grief can be released more easily. If, over time, we manage to look beyond the suffering, we discover many existential dimensions in grief and how loss and grief also loan clarity to life and love, force us to look at the meaning and purpose of our lives, and ask us to step deeper into our existence. By daring to look at life as it really is—full of loss, challenges, and adversity—we can create change, inner maturity, and strengthened awareness of our existence.

We therefore hope that the IPM can contribute to increasing awareness of and respect for our grief reactions, moving us away from undermining each other's ways of living with grief. The IPM offers a framework for us to instead look at loss as something that is existentially given and grief as a shared human experience through which we can find ways to help each other honor our losses, express our grief, and eventually grow into a deeper existential awareness, more human connectedness, and vitality.

Central points in Chapter 1

- Loss and grief are a part of every human life, and when we lose something that is most precious to us, the losses stand to us as the ultimate limitation of our human existence.
- Grief is always a form of love and the price we pay for love.
- Loss and grief are not just about death; they can be about all our connections to the world, everything that matters to us.
- The gap between what we want in life and what we now have lost creates a tension or a space in which we must now make changes and look for meaning. This gives us a basic existential tension or suffering.
- Because loss and grief are universal, all humans are united in loss and grief.
- Only the griever can tell us, what is lost and what grief is about—and how much grief is appropriate for them.
- The awareness of all the different losses in our lives can help us connect with ourselves and find a deeper understanding of our existence.
- In this book, we present a new, holistic and integrative model for loss and grief: the Integrative Process Model for Loss and Grief.
- Grief opens up a space for life's big questions full of tensions and paradoxes. There are no definitive answers here but more or less authentic ways of dealing with one's own existence.
- The four ultimate concerns in life that are central to this book are: the realization that we are mortal and will die ourselves one day; the question of what I do with my basic freedom as a human being; the fear of being alone and isolated from the rest of humanity; the search for a meaningful life.
- The question "What is the meaning of my loss?" cannot be answered by anyone other than the questioner and not by reasoning or thinking but by living the question.

Chapter 2

The integrative process model of loss and grief

> **Text box 2.1   On joy and sorrow**
>
> In his famous book *The Prophet*, the Lebanese-American writer, poet, and visual artist Kahlil Gibran (1883–1931) has a beautiful chapter on joy and sorrow (Gibran, 1923/2019). He reflects on how we all desire to have a life full of joy and without any sorrow. He uses the image of sorrow carving out a space in our being but that the same space is able to contain joy. When we reflect on the events that bring us deep sorrow, we will discover that they are connected to what brings us deep joy in life. Our whole life is suspended between joy and sorrow.

Developing a grief muscle

Just as Kahlil Gibran expresses it in the poem about joy and sorrow, in the course of our lives, we will experience many joys but also many losses. When the small joys and losses in life are not acknowledged, we overlook important aspects of our existence. What is even worse, when we do not acknowledge the many different losses we have over the years and the small, manageable losses we experience through a lifetime, we do not develop a natural language to talk about grief. We also do not train our ability to meet the big or defining losses in life. We do not get to build up a "grief muscle," which we would otherwise have the opportunity to do throughout life. Now we end up being completely stunned when loss strikes us.

When we then experience a central loss such as losing a loved one or a job or when illness strikes, we are overwhelmed by the pain and despair of grief, because we have not gained experience with grief. Subsequently, we flee from the grief when it strikes because the suffering of loss is intolerable, and we are completely unfamiliar with the pain.

DOI: 10.4324/9781003499060-2

While it is perfectly understandable to try to limit or avoid suffering, at some point, we may find that we spend our lives trying to escape any discomfort or pain. If we exhibited the same behavior in terms of training the muscles in our body, we would now no longer be able to lift a heavy load. If we do not train our "grief muscles" and develop a language around loss, we will only meet grief with disbelief and despair. Although loss and grief cannot be resolved, if we constantly run away from the pain of loss, we miss the opportunity to find a balance to live with the loss.

The answer to the pain is hidden in the pain itself.

For years, it has been called *working through* grief, as if there is an end to grief. The idea that we *come out on the other side* and can find a way to end the pain of grief suggests that there is a categorical answer to what to do with our grief. It suggests that there is a solution to grief. This implies that grief is a problem that we must solve. But there are probably very few people who experience grief as a problem that needs to be solved, let alone that the grief ends and we come out on the other side of it. However, studies show that we can reach a place where the grief becomes less painful or at which we find a way to contain the emotions and live with our loss (Nielsen et al., 2019). It has been said that it is as if grief asks us to have the courage to feel the pain in order to find a way to live with it. It does make sense that we must be in touch with the grief in order to find a way to adapt to the loss. Perhaps it can be compared to the body and mind feeling a new pain, and it takes some time to get used to this new strain and get to know it so that it can be integrated into life.

To be in contact with our grief is exactly the process that the Integrative Process Model of Loss and Grief (IPM) wants to depict. No matter how universal grief is, when we grieve, it quickly becomes clear that it is a very personal process for us. We might feel a calling or an existential ethical demand to honor our loss and take care of our grief.

When we experience loss,
we can come to a standstill,
or we can develop.

Irvin Yalom writes about the change in perspective and the existential awareness we develop over time with our losses.

Text box 2.2   The pleasures of sheer awareness

"There's a Schopenhauer quote that compares love passion with the blinding sun. When it dims in later years, we suddenly become aware of the wondrous starry heavens that had been obscured, or hidden, by the sun. So for me the vanishing of youthful, sometimes tyrannical, passions has made me appreciate the starry skies more and all wonders of being alive, wonders that I had previously overlooked. I'm in my eighties, and I'll tell you something unbelievable: I've never felt better or more at peace with myself. Yes, I know my existence is drawing to a close, but the end has been there since the beginning. What is different now is that I treasure the pleasures of sheer awareness."

(Yalom, 2016)

During that process, we will be confronted with life's fundamental existential tensions and thereby look deeper into our existence and perhaps ultimately work up more awareness.

Basic existential tensions in grief

The great existential tensions are part of every human life. But as we grieve, we are confronted with life's ultimate concerns such as death, loneliness, freedom, choice, responsibility, and faith. Therefore, IPM describes that in our grief, we become more aware of life's fundamental paradoxes and existential tensions.

Text box 2.3   The basic existential tensions in grief

1. The ultimate tension during grief is accepting death while embracing life. Only with the awareness of death will we get the most out of life, or even if we look at death, we have to want to live to find joy in life.
2. Another tension is dealing with our freedom to respond to our loss. On the one hand, grief is about being patient and letting grief and life unfold, and on the other hand, we must make choices while grieving and take responsibility for our grief. This can be called the paradox of doing or being. It's a battle that takes place in body and mind, and the question is how conscious we are of it.
3. A third important existential tension after suffering a loss revolves around our basic fear of aloneness. This tension is ignited by our tendency to feel alone after loss. On the one hand, we experience a fundamental separation from others and existential loneliness, and on the other hand, we fight for

connectedness and the feeling of belonging. So how do we strike a balance between holding on and letting go?

4. Finally, we are all suspended in a basic existential tension that is about finding meaning while feeling immense meaninglessness. We always have this tension within us, but it can be especially challenging when we are faced with loss. This tension is concerned with our basic search for meaning. How do we find a resonance in life that is solid enough to create a meaning that can carry our lives?

The ultimate concerns and existential tensions have previously been described in the work of existential therapy by authors such as Irvin D. Yalom (1980), Ernesto Spinelli (2005), and Emmy van Deurzen (van Deurzen & Adams, 2016). Central to this thinking is that as we live and grieve, we are confronted with questions that have no specific answers or solutions. The existential tensions and paradoxes are a fundamental part of the grieving process and of human existence, but at the same time, they are not problems that can be solved or removed. There are no specific coping strategies that will ease our existential anxieties. And while the existential tensions may torment us, there is no one who can heal them. What we can do, and what an existentialist would advise us to do, is to take responsibility and try to be brave enough to reflect on them. This is brought into the integrative approach to grief so that the existential tensions can help us balance our existence when it is filled with loss and grief. When we do this, we will discover that grief, despite the despair and suffering, also can become an opening to connectedness with ourselves and a deeper understanding of life and how we can live it (Cooper, 2003).

The IPM has been developed on the basis of various scientific and philosophical approaches to loss and grief. To better understand how the model attempts to integrate previous understandings and approaches to grief, let's first look at the understanding of loss and grief over the past century.

Standing on the shoulders of the different understandings in grief research

The scientific understanding of loss and grief has expanded and deepened significantly over the past decades. Traditionally, grief research has revolved around central themes such as: Who is grieving? How was the relationship with the deceased? How can grief best be described? What does grief look like in society/culture and in social processes? How do we deal with it when we grieve? What does normal versus complicated/pathological grief look like? What are the consequences of grief? and What can grief counseling or interventions look like, and what effect do they have? (Guldin & Leget, 2023).

Over time, research on grief has improved, and creative methods and innovative techniques have tested the basic assumptions we have held about grief. New theoretical models have been presented, and significant progress has been made in supportive interventions (Stroebe et al., 2008; Steffen, 2023). Our traditions and rituals of mourning and memorial practices have developed from private mourning to collective mourning practices with considerable cultural variation, such as memorial processions, lights in public squares, and virtual mourning on the internet (Rumbold et al., 2021; Walter, 2008, 2020). All this scientific knowledge about grief is embodied in theoretical models about our reactions to grief (also called stages), our handling of grief (models about tasks in grief), and the course and consequences of grief (models about pathological grief and diagnosis) (Stroebe et al., 2001; Milman, 2022). The theoretical models are placed within conceptual frameworks, research traditions, and paradigms, which depict our assumptions and understandings but also end up influencing and guiding our practice and further research.

If we look at loss and grief from a holistic and integrated perspective, we can ask ourselves whether our models of understanding provide satisfactory and adequate representations of the multifaceted forms of loss we experience in human life and the universality of grief. This plays a crucial role in how we understand the grieving person and how we support each other.

A brief visit to the understanding of the phenomenon of grief over time

Historically, there is a long tradition of literature about grief, suffering, and consolation within both philosophy and theology until the beginning of the 20th century. Yet the focus for understanding loss and grief shifted to be dealt with mainly within the discipline of psychology. Since Sigmund Freud published his classic and highly influential work *Mourning and Melancholia* in 1917, theories of loss and grief have been developed mainly within the disciplines of psychiatry and psychology. After this first systematic analysis of grief (Freud, 1917/1957), it has continued to occupy researchers all the way through the last century about how to deal with grief in human life.

Text box 2.4   Freud developed a hypothesis about grief work

Freud formulated a hypothesis that it is important to let go of the emotional bond with the deceased in order to adjust to life without the deceased. This meant that the mourner had to work with the grief and release the emotions surrounding the loss. Therefore, this hypothesis has later been called the grief work hypothesis. Later, Freud wrote about a changed understanding of the hypothesis of grief work, but the idea of working with one's grief and letting go of the tie to the deceased lived on in later models.

In the development of grief research immediately after Freud, the theoretical framework was still within a Freudian or psychoanalytic tradition. But gradually, the research became more grounded in systematic studies of mourners and representative studies on reactions and consequences of grief. This is represented, for example, by the English psychiatrist Colin Murray Parkes's influential work *Bereavement: Studies of Grief in Adult Life* (Parkes, 1972). This gave way to the exploration of complications in the grieving process, which was guided by theoretical understandings such as the attachment to the deceased and phase and task models of grief. In this period, researchers such as Elisabeth Kübler-Ross, John Bowlby, and William Worden became influential (Bowlby, 1980; Kübler-Ross, 1969; Worden, 1991) with different models about phases and tasks in the grieving process. See text boxes 2.5, 2.6, and 2.7.

Text box 2.5   Kübler-Ross's stages

Elisabeth Kübler-Ross's book *On Death and Dying* was published in 1969. Here, she listed five stages that we go through when we grieve:

1. Denial
2. Anger
3. Bargaining
4. Depression
5. Acceptance

Although these stages are still widely used in the understanding of grief, research has shown that these five stages are not universal in all grieving processes. They should therefore not be understood as a recipe that we can follow in grief.

Text box 2.6   Worden's grief tasks

William Worden published his book *Grief Counseling and Grief Therapy* in 1991. He presented four tasks that must be solved in grief:

1. Accept the reality of the loss
2. Work through the feelings of grief
3. Adapt to everyday life without the deceased
4. Emotionally relocate the deceased and move on in life

Worden's four tasks have played a central role in understanding how mourners can deal with grief. His tasks were almost understood as a recipe for how to grieve. As grief research has expanded the idea of what grief is about, Worden's approach to grief has also been understood as somewhat narrow.

By the turn of the millennium, research into the grieving process had become even more sophisticated. The complexity of grief was reflected both in the theory of human attachment, where the understanding of grief is a reflection of the attachment to the deceased person, and cognitive stress theory, where grief is understood as a stress factor that we have to deal with. On this basis, the continuing bonds theory by Klass et al. (1996/2014; text box 2.7), as well as the dual-process model (DPM) by Stroebe and Schut (1999, 2010; text box 2.8) and the theory of grief as construction of meaning by Neimeyer (2001; text box 2.9), introduced and started what can be called a new paradigm in the understanding of grief process and grief intervention.

Text box 2.7   Continuing bonds theory

The theory of continuing bonds or the continuation of the emotional bonds was published in 1996 by psychologist Dennis Klass and colleagues. The theory is that grieving people continue the emotional bond with the deceased by doing memorial activities, keeping things from the deceased, and other actions that maintain a sense of having the deceased close. The theory does away with Freud's grief work hypothesis and shows that we do not put grief or the feeling of connection with the deceased behind us but, instead, maintain the connection in grief. This understanding revolutionized the understanding of grief and continues to enjoy widespread support among professionals.

Text box 2.8   The dual process model on dealing with grief

The dual process model was published in 1999 by psychologists Margaret Stroebe and Henk Schut. They understand grief as a stress factor. Grief is a two-track coping process that oscillates between loss-oriented grief work and restoration-oriented focus on life changes. The oscillation between the two tracks provides a dynamic process toward integrating the loss into everyday life.

Text box 2.9   Meaning reconstruction

Psychologist Robert Neimeyer heads the Portland Institute for Loss and Transition. He explains that when we lose someone close to us, we lose our grip on the meaning of life. Grief is about reaffirming and constructing meaning in life after the loss. The model of construction of meaning is based on a constructivist tradition and describes that grief is about the mourner creating meaning in what happened via (a) what happened around the loss, (b) a deeper understanding of the relationship between the mourner and the deceased, and (c) the new understanding of the mourner's life (Neimeyer, 2001, 2011, 2023).

While the theories about the understanding of grief were reformulated around the turn of the century, all the attention around grief shifted from being taboo and a private matter to dealing more with the cultural context of grief, a new societal openness and public mourning with collective mourning rituals and the building of compassion in communities and society (Aoun et al., 2022; Walter, 1994; Doka, 2023). Now, the understanding of grief reflected that it is an individual process that follows many different courses, phases and tasks based on the circumstances surrounding the death (sudden/after long illness) and that depends on personal resources to arrive at an overall understanding that grief has no clear end but rather a dynamic and ongoing adaptation to the loss.

Subsequently, a large part of grief research and the understanding of grief in the 21st century has revolved around themes such as the duration and severity of grief, and especially the processes that have been called pathological have received a lot of attention. Many resources have been used for studies to establish criteria and name a diagnosis about the complications that can befall us when we are grieving, which concerns an estimated proportion of the population of 3% to 10% (Bonanno et al., 2011; Lundorff et al., 2017; Prigerson et al., 2009; 2021; Shear, 2015). In 2018, the World Health Organization (WHO) published a new international classification of diseases, ICD-11, which included the diagnosis of prolonged grief disorder (Boelen & Lenferink, 2020; Prigerson et al., 2009; Shear, 2015, Stroebe & Schut, 1999; van Heck & de Ridder, 2008). Since research into the pathological expression of grief has gained momentum, the focus and interest around grief has largely been on mental health, assessment of the bereaved's coping with grief, and setting up criteria in validated scales to find and help the approximately 7% with grief disorder.

Text box 2.10   The diagnosis of prolonged grief disorder

Prolonged grief disorder is a diagnosis established by the World Health Organization in the International Classification of Diseases, ICD-11. The condition is characterized by symptoms of a pervasive grief reaction with persistent emotional pain, persistent preoccupation, and missing the deceased. The disorder creates clinically significant functional impairment and difficulties in adapting to the loss. (Killikelly & Maercker, 2018)

The new diagnosis has been accompanied by a wide range of new, sophisticated psychological interventions and a diversity of approaches to grief and therapeutic initiatives around grief support (Aoun et al., 2012; Iglewicz et al., 2020; Johannsen et al., 2019; Steffen, 2023; Wagner et al., 2020).

Text box 2.11   Grief therapies

Today, there is a rich diversity of grief therapies with many different theoretical and philosophical roots (Steffen, 2023). The grief therapies have shown a good effect in terms of alleviating symptoms of grief disorder. Cognitive approaches in particular are dominant, and specifically, a therapy for prolonged grief disorder (prolonged grief disorder therapy) has shown good effect through several studies.

However, there are also many other psychotherapeutic methods such as narrative therapy, online offerings, and writing exercises that appear to be helpful. A pluralistic approach thus appears to be valuable.

There are still few studies of the effect of the various grief therapeutic initiatives as well as the patient associations' grief support and bereavement group services. But when looking at the systematically examined grief therapy offers, the most dominant models of grief that are used in the interventions today are the continuing bonds and dual process models (Fiore, 2021; Steffen, 2023).

There is a need to move the understanding of loss and grief forward

Although the understanding of grief has developed significantly in recent decades, there are three observations in particular that give food for thought (Guldin & Leget, 2023).

1. First, in current research and in the theories and models that are used today, grief is most often understood as something about losing a loved one to death.

Although we have shown earlier in the book that we experience many different losses in life, and grief is about many other losses than death, this is not properly reflected in the theories and models that are used to understand grief.

2. Second, the most dominant models of loss and grief have all been developed within psychological research. Over the years, this has resulted in a relatively large amount of literature with a focus on complicated and pathological forms of grief, since psychology is concerned with mental illness and its treatment. This focus can easily make us forget that 90% of grievers are not confronted with complicated or pathological processes but experience grieving processes which are natural. Hence, it is the far greater part of grieving processes that is currently not being researched that much.

3. Third, the dominant psychological approaches and models understand grief as a psychological process, as a stress reaction, and as a psychological distress, and they thus completely overlook the existential dimension of loss and the extensive impact that grief has on our existence.

Taking these three limitations into account, it becomes apparent that a more holistic model of grief is lacking that can reflect that loss and grief are also forms of existential suffering that every human being will experience and must learn to bear or live with. To be representative of all grief reactions, a grief model would have to reflect that grief is not only a phenomenon that we must seek to confront, deal with, or fix as a problem but also show that grief is a place where we reflect on the basic questions in life and looking for a position in the world. Until now, the models of understanding grief have failed to reflect the totality of the challenges faced by the bereaved and especially the existential concerns that arise due to grief. One could even claim that the basic existential suffering of the griever has been systematically overlooked in the models. When models of multidimensional phenomena such as grief become mono-disciplinary and reductionist, the research questions will become too narrow, and we will not notice that we fail to see the totality of the phenomenon we are researching. This may be precisely the reason that grieving persons continue to express feeling alone with their experience (Vedder et al., 2022; Vehling & Kissane, 2018).

In the integrated process model, the existential questions and tensions are moved to the forefront of the model to capture the experiences we have when we face a loss in life. The basis of the model is that the big existential questions become a kind of opening or entrance to our reactions to loss and grief and must therefore be included in the model.

The development of the integrative process model (IPM)

In the past four decades, many different approaches, theories, models, tools, and therapies have been developed about loss and grief. At first glance, it may even seem that everything in the grieving process has already been said or mapped. However, what has been lacking until now is a way to bring these insights from different disciplines and approaches together. This has precisely been the intention in the development of the integrative process model.

Gathering existing knowledge about loss and grief is not an easy task, however, as knowledge about grief comes from different sciences and with different forms of knowledge. Some of this knowledge is very concrete and close to practice, while another part of the knowledge is very abstract and stems from primarily existential and phenomenological thinking. Naturally, one should not compare apples with pears or make a mess of the scientific solidity on which the model is built. So in order to work on integrating knowledge, four levels of abstraction can be distinguished, according to which the existing scientific knowledge about grief can be organized (Guldin & Leget, 2023):

1. At the most practical level of grief, there are therapies, interventions, tools, and instruments that are used in the treatment and care of the bereaved (Steffen, 2023).
2. The practical level is supported by a more theoretical level, in which models of grief appear, such as the continuing bonds theory (Klass, 2006), the dual process model (Stroebe & Schut, 1999), or the model for meaning reconstruction (Neimeyer, 2023). The models constitute a concise representation of certain dimensions of grief, which are dealt with on a practical level in the therapies and tools.
3. The models of grief are based on an even more abstract theoretical understanding of grief developed in a mono- or multidisciplinary context, like the psychodynamic or cognitive behavioral therapy traditions within psychology. Here, for example, the dual process model is built on cognitive stress theory.
4. Finally, at the most abstract level, these theories are based on a specific scientific paradigm in which the nature and basis of a certain type of knowledge is defined, such as the natural sciences, social sciences, or humanities. Within and between these paradigms, different disciplines have developed their understandings of grief. For example, the dual-process model is based on research and developed on the basis of scientific principles.

There are good reasons there are different paradigms, disciplines, and theories of grief, because complex phenomena are best studied using appropriate scientifically sound methods. At the same time, it also makes sense that there is a wide range of therapies, interventions, tools, and instruments to serve the great diversity of needs of people with very different forms of loss and grief. When the different knowledge traditions have to come together to create a space in which insights from different disciplines are brought into conversation with each other, there is a risk that the fundamentally different insights from the different paradigms, disciplines, and theories lose their solidity. On the other hand, therapies, instruments, and tools are too specific to combine without losing their effectiveness. In our view, it is level 2, the level of models that allows opening a space for conversation, at which the research and thinking of different disciplines and professions can meet. Fortunately, there is a solid basis for developing such a model with all the work that has already been done on loss and grief reactions.

Total grief

Looking at grief research as a whole, grief is a process that develops physically, psychologically, socially, and existentially. Therefore, the model of loss and grief has been developed so that it can reflect the wide range of losses that occur in a lifetime and illustrate that loss is a fundamental, existential experience that is part of every human life and that affects all dimensions of our lives. The fundamentals of the model therefore had to be that grief has physical, psychological, social, and spiritual-existential dimensions. To develop this idea, the *total pain model was* used as inspiration, as it precisely aims to incorporate all professional disciplines into the understanding of suffering.

Text box 2.12   The total pain model

In the early 1960s, Dame Cicely Saunders, founder of the modern hospice movement, coined the concept of "total pain," suggesting that pain has a physical, psychological, social, and existential-spiritual component. The combination of the different dimensions of pain results in the total pain experience. Total pain is individual and specific to anyone in a particular situation. It is critical for health professionals to understand that a person's pain experience is always made up of physical, psychological, social, and spiritual-existential dimensions. In order to understand a person's pain and to be able to remedy the pain, it is necessary to study the different dimensions of the pain (Clark, 1999; Brant, 2017).

In order for a new grief model to describe all the processes in connection with the loss, the model is inspired by the model of total pain. In order to

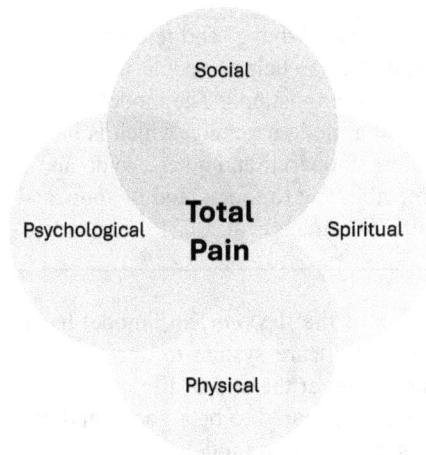

Figure 2.1 The total pain model: the four dimensions of total pain depicted as four overlapping circles: the physical, psychological, social, and spiritual.

illustrate and honor the existing grief research, it was decided to further refine the approach by distinguishing between the emotional and the cognitive dimensions of the processes in the psychological dimension. In the IPM, the processes are therefore divided into five dimensions, which can be distinguished when the previous research on reactions to loss is reviewed: physical, emotional, cognitive, social, and spiritual.

Although the IPM aims to integrate and connect different forms of knowledge that have been proposed in previous models, the model explicitly takes the grieving person's perspective as its point of departure. Loss is a common and natural experience that all people know and share. Yet grief is also a completely unique and personal experience because it is rooted in the specific loss of love, meaning, value, or connectedness in life that the griever has suffered. At the same time, it is closely connected to the griever's identity, core values, and past and planned future. This makes grief a deeply existential experience. Therefore, the IPM was developed as a model that illustrates that grief is something that can be understood as a unique and very significant experience for the individual. Finally, grief comes with a fundamental opportunity to open the fundamental existential tensions of life, which can lead us deeper into existential awareness and change.

To satisfy our basic assumptions about loss and grief as an existential experience, the development of the framework in the IPM used a skeleton of an old, classical existential model that presents the basic human tensions when facing death and loss, known as *Ars moriendi* or *the art of dying* tradition (Bayard, 1999; Girard-Augry, 1986; Laager, 1996). In the *Ars moriendi* model, there are fundamental existential tensions.

Text box 2.13   *Ars Moriendi*—the art of dying

Ars moriendi means "the art of dying" and refers to an old Christian tradition which, over the centuries, has helped people navigate the existential challenges and losses when life must end. The model is used in, e.g., the Netherlands and Belgium in a modern version which is based on five existential tensions: connectedness to oneself and others, to do and to let be, to hold on and to let go, to remember and to forget, and to know and to believe (Leget, 2007, 2008, 2012, 2017; Lormans et al., 2021; Vermandere et al., 2013, 2015).

The modern adaptation of the *Ars moriendi* model has been shown in studies to be very useful in the healthcare system to uncover existential questions that caregivers are confronted with at the end of life and loss and grief (Haufe et al., 2022). The model therefore appeared to be a good candidate to provide the basic architecture for the integrated process model.

The integrative process model of loss and grief (IPM)

The integrative process model illustrates grief in five dimensions: the physical, emotional, cognitive, social, and spiritual dimensions. Each dimension is linked to an ultimate concern and an existential tension characteristic of that dimension. Each dimension also has a number of key points of orientation that are important for finding a balance and living with the loss.

In the physical dimension, for example, there are various physical reactions to grief, such as stress hormones, restlessness, loss of appetite, fatigue, etc. In the emotional dimension, there are all the reactions that can be characterized as emotional, such as despair, longing, anger, and many more. In the cognitive dimension, reactions are described regarding our thinking and construction of meaning in grief. In the social dimension belong all reactions that have to do with our relationships, loneliness, and connectedness as well as cultural rituals. Finally, the reactions in the spiritual dimension are about aspects such as faith, guilt, shame, trust, and hope. Each dimension is elaborated in Chapters 3 through 7.

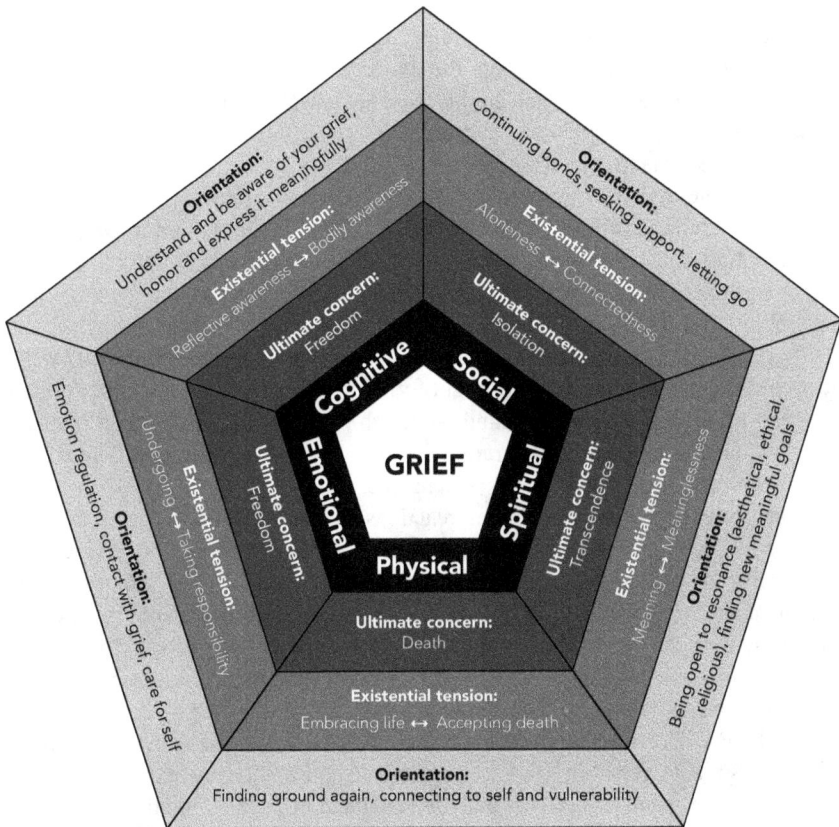

Figure 2.2 The integrative process model of loss and grief: the five dimensions of the IPM depicted as a pentagon, with each segment containing one dimension of grief with its central ultimate concern, existential tensions, and orientations.

The internal logic of the IPM is that the dimensions are inextricably linked,
but in order to understand and explore them,
the different processes are described based on these dimensions.

The model does not depict reactions or symptoms of grief but rather presents the challenges we face around loss in life within each dimension. The model also visualizes how grief opens up a space in which life's ultimate concerns and big questions become apparent, creating fundamental existential tensions that each individual must navigate through life. The fundamental existential dilemmas are illustrated in each dimension by showing the tensions that the griever is confronted with while struggling to balance all the reactions that grief causes. At the same time, in a dynamic movement, the griever tries to navigate the grieving process intrapersonally and interpersonally toward integrating the loss into everyday life and living an authentic life. At various times during the grieving process, one of the dimensions may come to the fore because of the reactions that characterize grief at that particular moment, and then, the existential tensions characteristic of that dimension also become relevant. In this way, the grief's reactions, challenges, and existential tensions change in a dynamic process toward living with the loss and the grief without ever landing definitively.

For example, it is a challenge in the physical dimension how to stabilize the acute grief reaction and the initial stress reactions immediately after the loss and regain footing and balance in the body's reactions. Another challenge, which is often mentioned in the emotional dimension, is illustrated as the regulation of one's emotional reactions during a grieving process, while other responses and challenges are associated with the cognitive, social, or spiritual dimensions. While these challenges are figuratively brought forth in each dimension, the other dimensions remain more in the background, although they are still present and relevant. This now becomes a way of illustrating the grieving process and its different reactions and processes in the different dimensions.

In the grieving person, the different reactions and challenges come alive in different ways in a very individual process. This creates a unique grieving process for each grieving person despite the commonality and universality of grief. The existential tensions pave the way for each griever to experience slightly different challenges; even if the existential tensions are the same for us, they will pose slightly different challenges for each individual during a grieving process. Our struggles with the existential tensions are also based on individual background, our loss, identity, values, and much more. So although the dimensions, the ultimate concerns, and the existential tensions are universal in grief, it is a personal and unique process how the challenges of grief present themselves and are navigated in the individual person. In the social dimension, the ultimate concern is, for example, aloneness, and the existential tension is about letting go but also holding on to connectedness. With our different backgrounds, resources, and cultures, we navigate the tension differently, but the universal process is that we all struggle with both being true to ourselves and being connected to others. In this process, the ultimate human concerns of death, freedom, aloneness, and meaning become prominent, and although they cause existential struggles and suffering, the central challenges or tasks we experience in the grieving process help balance and regulate the tensions.

In the understanding that life is always a tension between love and loss, grief and gratitude, suffering and meaning, the pain of the grieving process becomes a struggle and a useful orientation point at the same time.

A large number of studies on grieving processes have mapped the many factors that interact to give the grieving process an individual appearance. This concerns, for example, the meaning and experience of the loss, personality, previous experiences, and resources. According to the IPM, however, what is common to all grieving processes is that the five dimensions and the existential tensions are involved in one way or another. What is unique to all grieving processes is the specific way and order in which the processes in these dimensions unfold in the individual.

An important point is that the existential tensions that characterize the five dimensions of the IPM are in many ways consistent with previous work done in psychological research and even with the idea of oscillating between different aspects of grief, as pointed out in the dual process model. The difference, however, is that in the IPM, the polarities and tensions are understood as fundamental to all existential processes in life and not just arising in the psychological dimension or when trying to deal with a stressor. In other words, the existential tensions and challenges are already known to the individual, but when we grieve, they will be experienced with greater pressure and make demands on the person. Different tasks and central issues in the grieving process were already defined in Worden's phase model and in the dual process model (Stroebe & Schut, 1999, 2010; Worden, 1991). In the IPM, these insights are integrated in a more comprehensive way so that they include all of life's various losses, and the reactions and challenges are experienced within the physical, psychological, social, and spiritual realms, while the tasks that face the person in the grieving process are inextricably linked with the basic existential concerns and tensions that are always present in human life.

Last but not least, when complications arise with processing or integrating grief in the individual griever, support and treatment are naturally in their place, which has also been shown in much grief research (Guldin et al., 2017; Prigerson et al., 2021; Shear, 2015). This has recently also been described in a review of interventions made by, e.g., Robert Neimeyer (Neimeyer et al., 2023). As is also evident from the research literature, these types of loss and grief reactions are a minority of all the grief reactions described. Here, the IPM aims to encompass all loss and grief processes that we go through as humans and not just describe the pathological ones. The IPM could perhaps rather be described as a model for the prevention of pathology, since with its various dimensions, it illustrates the grieving process from the moment the loss occurs (acute grief) until the many challenges and existential tensions of grief have found a balance (integrated grief). The IPM therefore implies that support for the griever can take place throughout the grieving process, both as a prevention of complications and as support for the grieving process well into the process. However, it is not necessarily a matter of professional support.

Central points in Chapter 2

- Although it is a natural reaction to flee from pain and grief, it is important to train ourselves and build a "grief muscle" to deal with loss and grief.
- Grief is not something we go through and leave behind; when we learn to integrate the pain in our life, we can deepen our existential awareness and develop our vitality.
- Loss is an "existential earthquake" that exposes and makes visible the existential tensions and paradoxes in life that are fundamental to our existence.
- These tensions and paradoxes cannot be resolved. They present themselves as big questions or dilemmas in life. For example, how can I live when my loved one is so ill?
- By becoming aware of existential questions, you can learn to become more aware of yourself and the meaning of the life you live.
- Grief research started with Freud's classic book on Mourning and Melancholia, where the central idea was that it is necessary to give up attachment to a deceased person in order to adapt to the loss.
- Freud's thought has been carried forward in influential models such as Kübler-Ross's five stages and Worden's task model.
- The continuing bonds theory and the dual process model have nuanced the previous ideas about grief.
- Three observations underlie the integrated process model: (1) most theories of grief are too narrow and mainly connect grief with death; (2) most of the research has taken place within a psychological frame of reference and focuses on pathological forms of grief, which concerns less than 10% of mourners; and (3) the existential understanding of loss and grief is underdeveloped and not integrated into the grief models.
- The integrative process model (IPM) is a multidisciplinary model inspired by the total pain model from palliative care and is based on five dimensions in the grief process: physical, emotional, cognitive, social, and spiritual dimensions.
- The IPM integrates the five dimensions of grief with existential thinking, meaning that the model illustrates how each dimension contains a central existential concern and tension.
- The existential tensions are not unique to the grieving process, and most mourners will probably recognize the dilemmas from other processes in life, but they become particularly evident during the grieving process.

Prelude: Meet Ann, a grieving woman

We will now introduce Ann. The intention is to take a closer look at her grief process using the integrative process model (IPM). We visit her grief process through the lens of the different dimensions of IPM and the concerns, tensions, tasks, and points of orientation that are at stake in her grief as a way of getting in closer contact with the model. Her story is based on the life stories of many different people and cannot be traced back to any existing individuals or perhaps to all existing individuals. Pieces of her story are inserted in the upcoming chapters and reflect the issues discussed in the chapters in question.

We met Ann at the Center for Grief and Existential Values after she had broken up with a boyfriend. The breakup was causing her a lot of grief, which surprised her, as she didn't think she had been happy enough about the relationship for it to make her so sad. Ann was a sales manager in a large company, she was in her mid-50s, and she suffered from sadness and mental anguish. She otherwise had what can be called a good career and was supported by friends and colleagues. Although she had had several romantic relationships throughout her life, she had never settled down with anyone and started a family of her own. The relationship that had just ended had not lasted more than a year, and Ann had also been busy while the relationship was going on. Friends and colleagues envied her for her freedom and independence. They admired her sense of control over her life and her success, which, among other things, enabled her to live in a gorgeous house by the water and enjoy at least three vacations each year. Ann loved to travel, and she always chose destinations that inspired her to experience something new. She also liked to buy beautiful things to bring home, which she used to decorate her house so that it reflected her sense of beauty and the good life. She liked to have friends over on weekends. All in all, Ann seemed to be living the kind of life many people would envy as she began to feel increasingly dissatisfied with her life. The breakup with her boyfriend gave her many more reactions than she had anticipated. She did not quite understand what was happening and thought it might be related to her age. Financially, she could arrange to retire in a few years, although she was not sure what she would spend her days doing if she was not working. She had a sense of loss or emptiness, but was it just about getting older? Was it the prospect of retirement that cast a shadow? Or was it about something else?

Chapter 3

The physical dimension.
Why me?

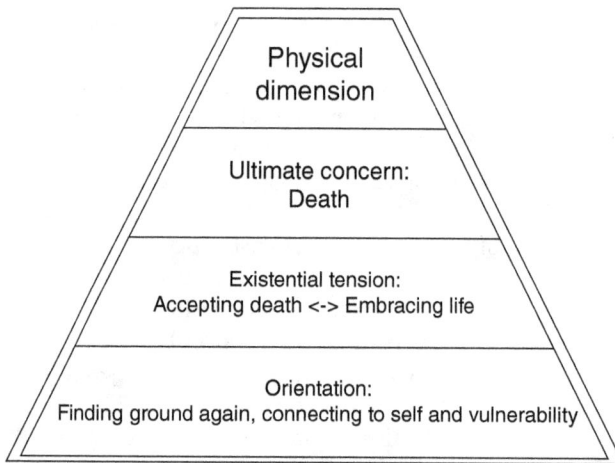

Figure 3.1 The physical dimension of the IPM depicted as the segment of a pentagon containing the ultimate concern of death, the existential tension
between accepting death and embracing life, and some orientations.

Viktor Frankl's autobiographical bestseller *Man's Search for Meaning* (1946/2006)
was based on his experiences as a prisoner in a concentration camp during World
War II. There, he suffered countless losses. The famous Brazilian writer Paulo Coelho was admitted to a mental hospital by his parents at the age of 17, as they apparently did not support his idea of becoming a writer. Coelho must have felt a great
loss in this lack of support and understanding. He tried to escape the institution. He
later started using drugs before having some sort of spiritual awakening and writing
his bestselling novel, *The Alchemist*, now translated into more than 80 languages
(Coelho, 1988/2014). The orphaned Harry Potter was conceived by J.K. Rowling,
who herself lost her mother at a very young age. Rowling ended up in more desti-
tution after a divorce and having to care for an infant alone with no job to support

DOI: 10.4324/9781003499060-3

them. Did these bestselling authors develop their success despite or because of their adversity? Another orphan, Cinderella, or even the Ugly Duckling gives us the fairytale of loss, but as in many fairy tales, adversity is turned around to build character and success. Just like many popular stories about superheroes, such as Superman, Batman, and Spider-Man, the basic human narrative tells us that through loss, we develop our identity and strength of character. Besides being instructive moral tales, these archetypal tales and basic human experiences open up a space in which we are confronted with life's great suffering and paradoxes, namely loss and death. No one is exempt from one day having to die and leave life. But as the Dutch philosopher Spinoza (1632–1677) said, "Each thing, as far as it can by its own power, strives to persevere in its being" (de Spinoza, 1677/1955). With this phrase, he opens up the possibility that despite adversity and suffering, there is a force within us that strives to become even more into being with the conditions we have landed in life with.

This chapter is about the physical dimension of the integrative process model and the big question *Why me?*

We grieve with our bodies

It is a widespread myth that grief processing only happens on an emotional level. In reality, our body also processes grief through our perception and senses, stress regulation in the nervous system, muscular tensions, and hormonal changes in our biochemistry. Acute grief, the grief immediately after the loss, is overwhelming and affects our entire body. Right after the loss, grief is often accompanied by loss of appetite, sleep disturbances, muscle tension, loss of energy, fatigue, and a wide range of other somatic symptoms such as nausea, dizziness, and aches and pains. For many mourners, the period immediately after a loss is therefore particularly characterized by dysregulation of the nervous system, now playing a major role in the grieving process while regulating tension and regaining biochemical balance in the body (O'Connor, 2019).

The earliest accounts of somatic responses to grief date back to Lindemann's descriptions in the 1940s of the responses following the deaths in the Cocoanut Grove nightclub fire (Lindemann, 1944). Although there is still a lack of knowledge in the field, there is no doubt that already in acute grief, physiological, biochemical, and neuropsychological factors play an enormous role in grief, and these bodily reactions can extend into a more persistent grief reaction. Numerous epidemiological studies of traumatic loss, morbidity, and mortality confirm the physical expression of grief (O'Connor, 2019; Boelen, 2015; Iglewicz et al., 2020). These studies indicate that the more sudden and traumatic the loss experienced, the more stress and increased levels of adrenaline are found in the body. This reaction can continue without regulation and cause higher levels of cortisol in the blood and dysregulation of the activity of the hypothalamic-pituitary-adrenal axis in the body. This means that there is now a risk of high blood pressure, dysregulation in the body's biochemistry, even higher blood markers of inflammation, and suppressed immune response. This can play a significant role in susceptibility to disease and even mortality after loss. Although these connections have not yet been fully mapped, it seems that the initial dysregulation in the body can cause major problems in the grieving process (O'Connor, 2019; Guldin, 2018).

In the IPM, an important part of a grieving process
is stabilizing the nervous system and regulating the somatic reactions
that naturally follow loss.

When the whole body is grieving, it is a prerequisite for grief processing that the body is stabilized and the nervous system works in a well-regulated manner. When the body has experienced a shock in connection with the loss because it was sudden or traumatic, this is sometimes called a peritraumatic reaction. Now, it is crucial to stabilize this and get a good foothold again before the body and mind can process the psychological aspects of grief, just like you need a firm grip when you are climbing a steep mountain. Stabilizing the body means regaining good sleep, hydration, nutrition, exercise, and relaxation.

After a loss, the body has to find a way to reduce the stress level
to be able to relax again, get sleep, and restore self-regulation.

Although it may feel as if the body is working against us immediately after the loss, the body's reactions to the loss are an important part of the grieving process that we cannot ignore. And it is in a coordination of senses, emotions, and thoughts that we can reconnect with ourselves after a loss. You might even say that the body is asking for it.

Finding your foothold again

The physical dimension of loss and grief is a natural part of the IPM regardless of the loss we have suffered. Here, it is described as central orientation points to stabilize the body or, as it is called in the IPM, to regain foothold. In the model, this captures the importance of the body being regulated, the necessity of being able to sleep, eat, and return to daily routines. This is done by listening to what the body needs. This equilibrium or balance is important so that the dysregulation in the body does not continue and opposes the grieving process. If this fails or we do not become aware of the imbalances in the body, there is a risk that the internal stress level or increased alertness will continue to create physical imbalances in the grieving process as we know it from anxiety or stress. If the body is out of balance, it requires energy and attention, and it is likely to complicate all the emotional, cognitive, and social processes of grief.

One of the things we do to create good contact with ourselves and balance in the body is actually quite simple: breathing. Breathing is the most fundamental basis for human life, and we breathe imperceptibly all the time. Right after suffering a major loss, however, even breathing can seem difficult. At the Center for Grief and Existential Values, we are sometimes asked by journalists how family members can help a grieving person, and we answer that actually, they can help the grieving person to breathe. We try to point out that we must all be aware of basic needs, slow down, and focus on specific aspects of the body's needs. That is to breathe, relax, sleep, eat, and even provide safety. Breathing can help us get in touch with our body and senses. For some reason, we don't talk much about this part of grief.

Listening to the body and feeling the body
is the start of healing the body
after a loss.

If we think that grief is purely a psychological or emotional challenge, we overlook the most obvious ways to help. We can easily overload our nervous system with emotional or cognitive problems while grieving. Restoring balance and self-regulation starts with listening to the body.

Exercise, fresh air, nature, art, and even contact with others
are also important parts of restoring balance when we are grieving.

The IPM emphasizes the need to physically stabilize the body and find a foothold in grief. From an existential perspective, it is quite common for bereaved people to struggle with regaining a sense of being connected to themselves and their own body again after the loss. It is essential to be in touch with ourselves to be able to deal with the big changes that loss can cause. This is the basis for finding a way to feel connected to life and to other people. Only when we have a sense of being well connected to ourselves and our body will we be able to integrate the loss into our lives.

Living the question: why me?

Right after the loss and during the process of finding foothold again, basic existential questions arise. One of the first questions we ask ourselves is usually: Why is this happening to me? How will I ever be able to live with this loss? Will I ever feel like myself again? Who am I now?

When you have suffered a significant loss, you are confronted like never before with the presence of death in life. The shock of the loss, its suddenness or unexpectedness, confronts us with all the limitations of our existence and accepting our place in the world. Paradoxically, this can create a big wedge between us and life, and now, we have to fight to restore interest in life. For example, when the loss is unexpected, sudden, or feels very unfair or out of the natural order of things, it is a struggle for us to feel anything but pain. We all have preconceived notions about right or wrong losses that we may not even be aware of until we are confronted with them. For example, many people find the loss of an elderly parent more tolerable than the loss of a sibling or child. The loss of an old parent can be understood as the "natural order of things," with the elders dying first and after having lived a long and fulfilling life. Studies show that our understanding of the loss and its naturalness affects our grief reactions and also the sympathy we show to other people in grief (Doka, 1989). The more unjust the loss is considered to be, the more grief we feel the person has a right to show and the more sympathy we show in return. These biases can become a struggle for the grieving person but ultimately also for ourselves in terms of accepting our own losses.

Text box 3.1   Existential reflection—unfair losses

- Try to take some time for an existential reflection to become more aware of your preconceptions about loss.
- Do you consider some losses to be more unfair than others?
- Does this also mean that you think some losses are fair? How would you describe these losses?
- Then try for a moment to imagine that you are the one who decides about losses in life. Would you then only inflict losses that you think are fair? And what would that mean for the world we live in?

Our preconceived notions about loss can mean that some losses are not recognized and supported, although this might not have any connection with the bereaved's own view on the loss and experience of pain. Professor emeritus Kenneth Doka, USA, writes about unrecognized grief termed *disenfranchised grief*. He describes losses that are not recognized or talked about and thus losses that are difficult to get support for. It can be loss of domestic animals, about an old grandmother, or about unrequited love (Doka, 1989).

Text box 3.2   Existential reflection—acceptable losses

Now, try to take the time for another existential reflection about your understanding of loss.

- Think about your own life and consider what losses you think have been natural and okay. And also think about what losses you have found unnatural and not okay.

- When you look at your own losses, what is the difference between the losses that you think are natural and acceptable and the losses that you think are unacceptable?
- Do they trigger different reactions in you when you think about them?
- What is a good way for you to think about your losses?

Doka appeals to us to become aware of our preconceived notions, both for our own sake and for the sake of the grieving people we meet (Doka, 1989). Only in this way can we begin to recognize and support each other's loss on the basis of the bereaved's own experience of the loss and what support they feel they need, and not on the basis of what we ourselves might think is a real loss.

Will modern man ever be able to accept
that death and loss disrupt our lives, plans, and dreams?

From an existential perspective, loss confronts us with our finitude and mortality, or what has been called the ultimate concern of death. This means that we are confronted with the fact that we all live and die, that someone we care about becomes ill, or that we do not feel that we are where we want to be and that life is not always the way we want it to be. No one can avoid disaster or loss in their life. It makes us feel powerless or very vulnerable, especially if we have never before faced or been forced to deal with our own vulnerability and the limitations of life.

Death, limitation, and annihilation are our ultimate fears
and can therefore easily become sources of existential anxiety and mental
suffering.

That is why the French writer François de La Rochefoucauld (1613–1680) wrote in one of his maxims that even if we know it exists, we cannot stand looking at it all the time.

"Neither the sun nor death can be looked at with a steady eye."
(de La Rochefoucauld, 1665/2008)

When you mourn one loss, you mourn all your losses

The American writer John Greene expresses in the moving book *The Fault in Our Stars*, which was later made into a movie, how grief has the quality to reveal who we are as human beings.

In many other novels and films, it becomes clear that when we grieve, it is as if fate invites us to a test of strength. The world seems different and new and contrasting to what we already know or have been confronted with before. This means that we question life. The questions can be about the fear of death or being alone, they can be about our struggle to take responsibility for our own choices in life, or even about what we believe and what or who we can trust. The questions present basic existential themes. They are related to this loss but also to experiences with former losses and suffering. Behind the current loss, past losses now appear, and our minds become occupied with these themes. Grieving individuals often report that they begin to think about past losses as if their bodies, emotions, and thoughts are being reminded of past loss experiences. It might be because the existential themes are similar for all the losses. This means that we might as well expect this. When we struggle with one loss, the bodily reactions, emotions, cognitions, neural pathways, our social behavior, and spiritual awareness seem to naturally come into contact with previous losses. This timelessness or temporality is described in several places in philosophy, sociology, and psychology by, e.g., the Swiss psychiatrist Carl Gustav Jung (1875–1961) and the American philosopher George Herbert Mead (1863–1931), explaining that we constantly understand ourselves based on this moment in time and recreate past events against the background of the construction we create in the present.

> In the wake of a current loss,
> we regrieve past losses
> because the existential themes are similar
> and work in us all our lives.

It can be a painful and overwhelming struggle, but it can also be seen as an invitation to deepen our understanding of an old loss, adapt it to the present, and help us into a deeper understanding of our lives.

> It is a widespread misunderstanding,
> that when we continue to mourn our old losses,
> it means we did not completely cope with them yet.
> It is more likely that it is because love never ended.

However, studies show that regrieving old losses is common and normal, especially when there are reminders of loss and grief, suggesting that regrieving plays an important role in our grief. Existentially, it would also make sense that we live in a continuous exchange with the world, constantly looking for how to respond to what happens and finding meaning in it, finding the balance between feeling alone and connected to others. Therefore, we can only understand one loss by understanding past losses. These are existential themes that are relevant again and again in our lives. Thus, one interpretation could be that our mind invites us to look at our past losses in life with the aim to try to understand them from a new perspective later in life. At the same time, knowledge from previous losses can provide valuable information about the new and current grief. Perhaps it can even produce insights from a new perspective based on the new experiences you have gained. From an existential point of view, this could even be seen as the current loss giving rise to basic existential questions in which we now seek a better balance, and therefore, it confronts us with the existential themes of our old losses. When we can learn from past existential themes, we can more easily find the right balance and be connected to ourselves, our life history, and our present. It can even be seen as a way of looking for our own authenticity in the situation.

Rather than thinking that the past losses get in the way of us being able to concentrate on the current loss, an existential interpretation could be that it can be useful to reflect on past losses and the role they play in our life story. Perhaps they brought us wisdom and insights. Past losses and old grief are therefore not something we have to fight or dismiss. They can help us understand ourselves and our values in life as well as aiding our search for existential meaning.

Text box 3.3   Existential reflection—being mortal

Go back in time and try to remember earlier losses you had.

- When was the first time you realized that loss is irreversible and that life would never be the same as before?
- How did it resonate with the awareness that life is finite?
- When was the first time you clearly felt that you are a mortal being?
- How did it make you feel? What did it evoke in you?

Every loss confronts us with our own death

In a famous letter to Countess Sizzo, the German poet Rainer Maria Rilke reflects on how death is a complementary part of life. Life and death have a indissoluble unity, which he expresses by using the image of the moon with its dark side that is turned away from us but is at the same time indispensable for giving the moon the shape of a perfectly round circle (Rilke, 1923/1949). Many well-known philosophers and thinkers have written about the connection between life and death and how they are not only each other's opposites but also each other's qualification. Just as there is no love without loss, there is no experience of loss that is not about some form of love, connectedness, or meaning.

> Love and loss qualify each other.
> One does not exist without the other.

In Stoicism, the ancient philosophical tradition, it is said that death is the most important experience in our lives. In the philosophy of existence, the famous German philosopher Martin Heidegger (1889–1976) explained that death is the horizon which allows us to reflect on our being and forces us to make choices and live authentically. Yalom is quoted for the idea that "Though the physicality of death destroys us, the idea of death may save us" (Yalom, 1980). In other words, awareness of loss and death changes our perspective on life and illuminates our priorities. So even if we would like to live life without loss, it is often in the wake of loss and death that we learn how to live life to the fullest.

When we experience loss, we are confronted with the limitations and finitude of life and even our own mortality. When we lose a spouse or loved one, the "us" we knew is gone. We have to reinvent ourselves in a changed world. With the "us" gone, the person we once were is now changed, and the person the deceased saw in us is also gone. At the Center for Grief and Existential Values, our experience is also that people who live with overwhelming losses, such as the loss of a child, not only experience the enormous pain and suffering, which grieving for the child is, but for most parents, it also affects the very feeling of being a parent and aspects such as facing the guilt because they have not been able to protect or save the child, regardless of how little they could have done to actually change the situation. These are also called secondary losses: losses that follow the primary loss of the child. Or take, for example, the grief we experience at the loss of public figures, artists, musicians, or royalty. This is sometimes called parasocial grief (O'Connor, 2022). We invest part of our identity in famous people, we use them as role models, and we even use their identity as our mirror, because while we follow their lives, they help us shape our own life and worldview. Therefore, the grief we feel when a public figure dies is a grief of losing a valued role model.

> When we experience a profound loss in life,
> then it is experienced as a loss of identity, of hope, and of direction in life.

Despite the tremendous losses we may suffer, most of us will go to great lengths to avoid looking at our own powerlessness. This also happens with living losses, such as the loss of a body part, a function, or a dream. The American philosopher Christine Korsgaard has coined the term *practical identity investment* for all the obligations, values, and concerns we embrace as human beings (Cholbi, 2022). Our commitments, values, and concerns help shape and give direction to our lives and instill a sense of integrity, and our practical identity can explain our crucial choices in life and give us a description of what we value in our lives. Naturally, other individuals and role models also play a central role in our practical identity. Being objects of admiration and love, they help shape our worldview, which becomes our identity. Existentially, the losses confront us with our own powerlessness, loss of control, isolation, meaninglessness, and ultimately, our own death.

Many great thinkers such as Heidegger and Yalom argue that death and loss teach us to live and find meaning, because when we are confronted with our own powerlessness and finitude, we take our own lives into consideration. Without death, we wouldn't bother enough. None of us knows what life would be like if it were infinite and we were immortal. Or if we would never feel sorrow or sadness. Although we may not be concerned with this particular aspect of death immediately after we have lost, the confrontation with death and loss over time teaches us a kind of humility or having to face the fact that at some point, we, too, will be struck by fate and lose something that for us is the essence of life.

> The power of loss is that it takes away our illusion
> that we are so special that we cannot die
> or that we will ultimately be saved by a supernatural power.
> This is also the moment where we can really begin to understand life.

Each and every loss in our path reminds us that we are mortal and our lives have limitations. This may not sit well with the modern narrative that each individual is unique and special and inhabits an invaluable place in life. Still, it becomes clear that the narrative of loss is that we do not have the right to decide everything in life, and some things are beyond our power and influence. Loss is a disruption in our life narrative; it affects our understanding of our physical being as it confronts us with our finitude and mortality.

Existentially, we must face the ultimatum of death. The concept of death is understood here in a broad sense, as something that refers to the finality of human life, i.e., to relationships, functions, roles, status, ideals, and ambitions, all of which play a role in shaping a sense of ourselves or our identity. Existentially, grief is a process that takes place in the shadow of our ultimate concern of being mortal. Everything in our lives has an expiration date.

Our struggle to surrender to loss

Text box 3.4   The story of a mother

There was once a mother who lost her child. She refused to accept that Death took her child. She spent her life chasing Death to get her child back. All the while, she walked a lonely road where no one could follow her. In the fight against Death, she lost her youth, her beauty, and her eyesight. Her grief was so intense and so blinding that she did not notice that she was also losing herself. Even when other people tried to tell her that Death never returns anything, she did not stop to reflect on it. Only in the moment when, in a fit of rage, she threatened to kill another child did she realize that grief had made her numb and blind. She had been unable to accept Death and relinquish her claim. Only after realizing what her fight against Death had turned her into did she learn to surrender and live with her loss.

(Source: H.C. Andersen, 1847/2020)

Hans Christian Andersen's (1805–1875) fairy tales are stories that express a deep understanding of life and contain existential wisdom. The story of a mother can be understood as a struggle against death, a complication of grief, or, as we might understand it today, even an example of a grief disorder. The remarkable thing is though that H.C. Andersen wrote the adventure in 1847, long before there was anything called grief disorder. Even then, he shows us that if we fight against acknowledging our loss and refuse to accept it or keep questioning why this had to happen to us, we can end up losing ourselves too.

In the IPM, the essential question "Why me?" is connected with the processes in the physical dimension. Here, the grieving process is characterized by the existential tension between *embracing life* on the one hand and *accepting death* on the other. This must be understood in both a concrete and an abstract way. As it says in the Bible: "For dust you are, and to dust you shall return" (Genesis 3:19). Accepting one's place in the world is also sometimes called humility. It has nothing to do with being humiliated or submitting to anything or being oppressed by a divine authority. It also has nothing to do with not standing by yourself and your own convictions. Rather, humility is associated with having realistic expectations about life and death. Central to the concept of humility is accepting that it is not up to us to decide who lives and who dies. This kind of humility can help navigate the tension between embracing life and being mortal and vulnerable. The more we are able to accept our finitude and mortality, the more we can live life without the fear of death and also begin to sense an answer to this eternal question related to loss and suffering: "Why me?"

In a religious mindset, decisions about life, death, and loss are ultimately not up to humans. This is also still the official position of the major world religions: Hinduism, Judaism, Christianity, and Islam. All the great world religions express a notion of death and loss, but here, the existential tensions and paradoxes of human life are placed in a larger story, where humanity is transcended by a God or by divine forces. The exploration of how different religious and nonreligious traditions (such as Buddhism and humanism) view loss and grief will be discussed briefly in Chapter 7. In all these traditions, we find a respect, awe, or reverence for the great mystery of life that transcends the human mind. The IPM is open to interpretation from both a religious and nonreligious framework, but in the model, the transition from life to death is seen as a process that not only confronts us with a human's unique value but also with aspects of our lives that we struggle with when becoming more aware of, for example, our relationship to death, powerlessness, and meaning.

Text box 3.5 Existential reflection—having power over death

- Who deserved to live and who deserved to die?
- And who should have the power to make such a decision?
- If you had the power to make these types of decisions, what would that responsibility mean for your life? What role would you then have?
- Do you know the feeling of longing for death? What does it tell you?

The physical dimension in the IPM opens up a tension between the polarities: facing death or loss and at the same time connecting us more to life. This tension can be very difficult to balance. Right after losing a loved one or something crucial in life, it is natural to experience being thrown or pulled toward the polarity of death. Our thoughts revolve around loss and death. Maybe we feel tired of life and have thoughts about longing for death or maybe, rather, that we do not want to be in life. Such a strong reaction can easily result in a wish for a hastened death. In this situation, the pole of death in the existential tension is so prominent that the pole of life seems to have completely disappeared. Yet at the same time, one can say that the ferocity of this reaction shows that there is still a lot of vitality in the person. This opens up a new perspective, namely that this is also an opportunity to move toward the desire for life. It is a process that takes time, but it provides an important hope.

What is *carpe diem* without *memento mori*?

Death is also a beginning.

In reality, balancing the tension between embracing life and accepting death is a challenge for every one of us every day. The tension and contrast just become very clear when we are confronted with death and finitude. Not only must we here seek connectedness to life despite death and loss, but we must also accept our own vulnerability and finitude. In our Western tradition, two proverbs are used to express this tension. The saying *Carpe diem* ("Seize the day") encourages us to live in the here and now and make the most of each day. Days come and go like flowers, so it is about watering them while they are there. The words *Memento mori* ("Remember that you will die") express the existential awareness of our finitude and that one day, we will have to let go of our earthly existence. Both proverbs express the tension between embracing life and accepting death, although they originate from different times and place the emphasis on human life differently. Only when seen in context can they help us navigate the physical dimension of grief. And only in context will they reveal the infinite depth of every moment we breathe.

Text box 3.6   Existential reflection—seize the day, but remember that you will die

- What would it look like if you could live each day without life ever ending?
- What does the saying "seize the day" mean to you?
- What does the saying "remember that you will die" mean for the way you live life?
- Does the meaning of the two proverbs change when you see them in relation to one another?

Wounds are eyes

In one of the beautiful texts ascribed to the Persian poet Rumi (1207–1273), there is a dialogue in which someone asks questions to gain wisdom. One of the questions is how to deal with the pain and sorrow that is found in our hearts. "Stay with the pain" is the advice for wounds are where the light can enter us: they are openings for new insights and wisdom (Rumi, 2024).

Human life is vulnerable. We may have an accident, be hit by a natural disaster, or our child may fall ill. Some people have a difficult start in life, for example, being subjected to poverty or a lack of support and love. Other people cannot get or achieve what they want in life, and a lifelong dream such as becoming a parent or marrying the love of their life is not fulfilled. We all suffer from feeling loss or limitations in our everyday life or career and many do not yearn for more recognition or perhaps personal possessions they had dreamed of. The German writer Jean Paul (1763–1825) wrote about "Weltschmertz," namely the pain that lies in realizing that the real world will never live up to the hopes and dreams our minds can imagine for us (Paul, 1846/1963). When this is linked to our understanding of ourselves, our identity, and something that feels unlived in our lives, we can easily experience it as a lifelong grief.

When we grieve, it is natural to feel that it is unfair that we must experience such a loss or even to believe that no one can understand the extent of our grief. This is a common and understandable reaction when we suffer, but it is also a form of black-and-white thinking that is not connected to reality. We divide the world into good and bad people or experiences, because when emotional reactions are over-whelming, this black-and-white worldview is easier to understand.

> We tend to think that some losses are unfair,
> but that would mean that other losses are fair.
> And which ones are they?

Who deserves to suffer loss and who doesn't—and who is to be the judge of this anyway? Life is not fair, and a divided worldview does not help us balance the tension between life and death. It simply neglects the vulnerabilities of our existence. Instead, black-and-white thinking is likely to cause even more struggle and pain. Let's try to explain why.

> When we divide the world into good and bad people or experiences,
> we risk becoming victims of our own adversity,
> for now, we constantly think that something unfair has happened to us.
> We have thus made ourselves victims, and from here, it is difficult to find a
>   balance in life.

When grief overwhelms us, it is very difficult to take responsibility for our thinking, and it is difficult not to project or transfer the hurt onto others. Especially the helplessness we feel can be projected with a lot of thoughts about what others do not understand, because then, we have shifted the helplessness to another person. What we overlook in that thinking is that each one of us has our own struggles, losses, and sufferings, and even though some have experienced more suffering than others, it will only feel good for a short while to divide the world into black and white, and then it creates new problems for us. Because nothing is unambiguously good or bad. This mindset that helped us in the beginning will now work against us and create problems in our thinking because it becomes distorted or one-sided. We disconnect, we cut ourselves off from the outside world, and we become rigid in our thinking rather than looking for resonance and connectedness with others. In the long run, black-and-white thinking will not help us, because it leads to a one-dimensional simplification of human existence. It is more useful to look for ways in which our shared vulnerability can unite us rather than divide us.

In English, vulnerability is derived from the Latin word *vulnus* ("wound"). Vulnerability means that there is a possibility of being hurt. In a figurative sense, you can say that the wounds in our body open the skin, which is the boundary between us and the world around us. This boundary defines our self and protects us, but it also closes us off and cuts us off from our surroundings. Wounds become a kind of painful openings in this delicate membrane, the skin, which surrounds us and makes us aware of our limits and our fragility. But every wound also brings bacteria with it and thus exchanges a kind of knowledge with the surrounding world.

> Wounds can be called eyes in the sense that
> they help us see or experience things
> we did not see or know before.

In this way, wounds can also be understood as an exchange that can strengthen us in the long term. This can make us wiser in terms of knowing what hurts but also teach us compassion for our own and other people's vulnerability. In the existential tension between *embracing life* and *accepting death*, we begin to realize that vulnerability is shared, as no one knows what will be lost tomorrow or who will be the next to suffer loss. In time, we can develop the courage to reconcile the fact that one day, we ourselves will suffer the ultimate loss and have to face death.

Vulnerability as superpower

In our Western culture, many feel that it is weak and shameful to show vulnerability or humility. We avoid showing how hurt or vulnerable we feel, and we refrain from asking for help or talking about the vulnerability. Instead, we spend our energy trying to show strength or pretend that everything is fine.

> Human finitude, our vulnerability and lack of control
> are overwhelming and painful experiences.
> But contrary to their bad reputation,
> they also force us to think about our own existence
> and how we can be connected to ourselves and life.

It is out of touch with the realities of human existence to think that vulnerability is not a part of every human life. When we face a great loss, it is hard to avoid feeling unfairly treated by life or shift our focus to what others cannot understand, talk about, or support us in. But that probably will not help us in the long run, since we cannot change other people but only our own approach. Existentially, it is our own attitude that can help us and whether we dare to face the loss. The existential tension between accepting death and embracing our life force pushes us toward realizing the nonnegotiable. Painful questions arise about how we can go on when life throws these devastating losses at us.

After a significant loss, we ask ourselves several existential questions. Throughout the existential tension between being given life through birth and having to leave life to die, some questions are eternal companions: Why is my life this way? How do I want to live my life? What gives meaning to my existence? You could say that these questions give rise to a feeling of vulnerability, but at the same time, they also capture our vitality. It provides loss with a potential to transform our lives if we seek to answer these existential questions.

Accepting vulnerability and even humility does not mean that we have to live our lives in the shadow of all the losses that may occur or our ambitions or ideals that do not come true. Accepting vulnerability means having the courage to accept our powerlessness, use it as experience, and still have the courage to take risks and live freely without being able to control the outcome—for example, daring to love again even though we have lost what we loved most. It is by daring to feel the vulnerability that we can meet others and bond with others even after a loss. It is precisely finding the balance between accepting death and embracing life. Vulnerability is the strength to admit to oneself that none of us has the power to control everything, and in this respect, we are all the same, for we share this vulnerability with the rest of humanity. Existentially, this means that we must all learn to dare to be open to the notion of loss and death. Only in this way can we navigate loss and grief and work to live with our loss but at the same time actively choose life and remain connected to our life force.

> To accept our vulnerability or finitude
> by feeling the connection to our mortal body
> also has the potential to put us in touch with our sensitivity and empathy
> and thus the quality with which we experience life.

This is a core strength, if not a superpower, as promised in the popular tales of superheroes and their losses.

Text box 3.7   The mountain range exercise on losses

Each and every one of us has already had many losses in our lives and accumulated a lot of experience with grief. The more aware we are of our own experiences of loss, the better we can draw on them as sensitivity, compassion, resource, and strength. The following exercise can help to practice awareness of one's own losses and one's own grief.

Imagine you are drawing a mountain range on a piece of paper. The mountains represent a timeline from your birth at one end until today. Each mountain in the mountain range represents a significant loss you have had in your lifetime. Write inside the mountains on the paper which losses you think of. It could be the loss of significant people in your life, a lost job, divorce, health-related losses, or functional losses. Also consider the loss of a pet, having to move away from friends as a child—in short, any major changes in your life and the losses they entailed.

Once you have placed the significant losses on your mountain range, go over the loss line again, and this time, reflect on how your losses affected you. Add some comments in the valleys between the mountains, where you now write some cues about how you reacted or how each loss affected you. It can also be secondary losses to the primary loss such as something missing in the connection with your parents or siblings, your experiences at school, relationships that did not develop as you wanted, or aspects of your life that you strongly desired but that did not materialize.

Finally, look at the mountain range one last time, and now, write your existential learning from each loss on each mountain peak. It can be aspects like being confronted with death, feeling abandoned, connectedness with a special friend, meaninglessness, a new value, etc.

Now consider the following:

- Are the losses in the mountain range connected in any way?
- How have the losses affected your understanding of life? Your dreams? Your values?
- What wisdom have you taken with you about loss and about life?

Central points in Chapter 3

- The physical dimension of the IPM is mainly about acute grief affecting our entire body and nervous system.
- The IPM describes how it is part of grief to stabilize the body, which is called "finding a foothold" and is about restoring sleep, good eating habits, and regular exercise.

- Footing starts with listening to the body and feeling the body and its needs.
- Taking care of our vulnerable body and accepting the pain can be the first step to finding our footing again.
- Every loss confronts us with our own vulnerability, finitude, and mortality: it confronts us with our own impotence and death.
- At the same time, it is death and the finitude of life that spur us to reflect on life and how we want to live it.
- The question "Why me?" can make us think about our own preconceived notions about loss and what a natural death is and who defines this.
- The existential tension in the physical dimension is described as a tension between embracing life (carpe diem) on the one hand and accepting death (memento mori) on the other.
- As we navigate life in the awareness of this inextricable tension, we embrace our vulnerability as mortals, and this can give our lives a deeper quality of experience.
- Our loss and grief can make us wiser to what really hurts in life, but at the same time, they teach us compassion for other people and our common vulnerability. It is called in this chapter a kind of superpower.

Interlude: Ann's struggle with the physical dimension of the loss

Ann came to the Center for Grief and Existential Values because of the grief after the failed relationship. She felt that she had lost her balance. She had no appetite, felt unhappy and tense, and did not go on the walks she normally enjoyed. We did a little visualization exercise with her:

Imagine you are standing on a wide, beautiful beach with an incredible view. Before you, the sun is about to go down. The sunset is impressive with flaming yellow and red colors. It was a beautiful day, and the sun shun on you with bright colors, it warmed you up and filled your senses and made you feel alive. Now, you are looking at the sun setting. Picture the sun slowly sliding below the horizon and disappearing until it is completely gone. It gives you a sense of deep sadness, and it feels colder, like a part of you is dying. The world is now different and darker. You miss the sun. But notice, in a short while, the night sky will emerge and reveal the most wonderful stars that also shine bright on you. Look up at them and the wonder they carry. Think about how many other people in the world look up at the same stars, maybe even sharing some of the same struggles and suffering. For a moment, feel the resonance and connectedness of that thought. And Ann, now, you realize that your sun is still there. Right now, it is hidden by the night sky, but it is important to take in that the sun is not gone. Maybe you can even transcend the feeling of warmth it gave to you and let this warmth shine as a beacon of hope. Because soon, the sun will rise again. It will be a different sun and a new day. Still, it will shine on you and once again give you warmth and make you feel alive.

Ann was surprised how much the loss of this relationship affected her, but she had also had thoughts about whether menopause made it more difficult for her. For the first time in her life, she felt how her body, which had always been very strong and needed very little sleep, was becoming unreliable and felt vulnerable. She suffered from hot flashes at awkward times during her work and sleepless nights that left her exhausted. There was a new sense of frailty in her body that made her tired and sensitive, and it was hard not to have control over this body that had always been such a strong companion for her. She discovered that it was affecting her in a deeper way than she had wanted to realize. We asked her to reflect a little with us on the choices she made in life and whether it was a conscious decision to not have a husband and children. Ann looked back on her life. When she was only a few months old, her mother died in a car accident. Her father had been driving the car after he had drunk too much. Although he survived the accident, he had to undergo a long rehabilitation. It turned out he had a hidden drinking problem, and his guilt made him a wreck. When her father was unable to care for her, Ann grew up with her aunt. During the times when she lived with her cousins, who were a few years older than her, Ann never felt completely welcome in the family. Her aunt made her feel like she was out of place. Ann remembered when she was little, she romantically identified with Cinderella, feeling unwanted in the world. She quickly learned that in the end, she could only rely on herself. Ann had a good head on her shoulders and developed into a very strong and independent person. She did not like the feeling of being vulnerable or lacking an identity in her family, so she had taken up an education, through which she could feel strong and get a foothold. She had worked hard to get a good position in life, and she enjoyed that her colleagues admired her for her strength and being true to herself. However, this new loss of a boyfriend and the symptoms of menopause left her feeling vulnerable and powerless. She realized that the end of life was closer than ever and that some things like having a family or even children would never happen, and somehow, that made her very sad and reflective.

Chapter 4

The emotional dimension.
What can I do?

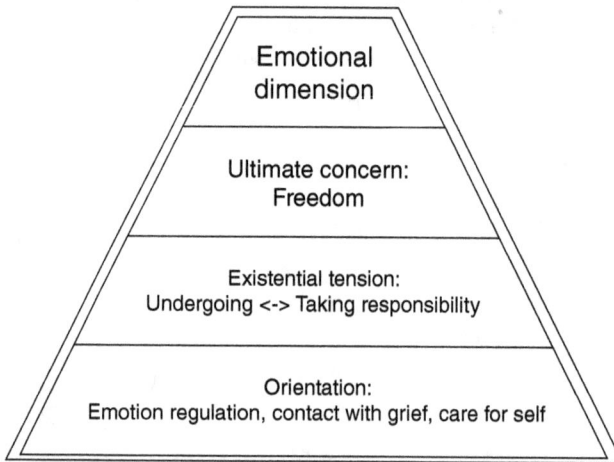

Figure 4.1 The emotional dimension of the IPM depicted as the segment of a pentagon containing the ultimate concern of freedom, the existential tension between undergoing and taking responsibility, and some orientations.

"God, give me grace to accept with serenity
the things that cannot be changed,
the courage to change the things
which should be changed,
and the Wisdom to distinguish
the one from the other."

Reinhold Niebuhr (1932)

DOI: 10.4324/9781003499060-4

Many readers may be familiar with a version of the Serenity Prayer, written by the American theologian Reinhold Niebuhr (1892–1971). For many people today, this prayer is about living with alcoholism, as the prayer became popular through Alcoholics Anonymous in the 1970s. But the thoughts expressed in the prayer are much older. The great German poet and philosopher Friedrich Schiller (1759–1805) wrote more than 200 years ago:

> "Blessed is he, who has learned to bear what he cannot change, and to give up with dignity, what he cannot save."
>
> Schiller (1796/1984)

And almost 2,000 years ago, the Greek philosopher Epictetus (c. 50–135 AD) wrote:

> "Make the best of what is in your power and take the rest as it happens. Some things are up to us and some things are not up to us."
>
> Epictetus (135/1983)

Originally, the Serenity Prayer also contained the words:

> "Living one day at a time,
> enjoying one moment at a time,
> accepting hardship as a pathway to peace,
> taking, as He did,
> this sinful world as it is,
> not as I would have it."
>
> Reinhold Niebuhr (1932)

Accepting adversity as a path to inner peace is a big challenge for most of us. There are probably not many existential experiences that have more potential to teach us the lesson of distinguishing between what we must accept and what we can work to change than when we experience loss. While grieving, it can take all of our energy and courage to understand and accept the loss of something valuable and meaningful. Grief takes time and patience. The reputable grief researchers and parents of the well-known dual process model, Margaret Stroebe and Henk Schut from Utrecht in the Netherlands, said many years ago in a speech when they held a course in Copenhagen (Personal communication, 2006):

Grief takes the time grief takes.

When we grieve, we can feel stretched thin between past and future and between the overwhelming pain of loss and acceptance of the reality of loss. When faced with so much pain, we naturally tend to try to avoid the pain and run away from it, or we ask ourselves the question: What can I do? In their psychological model of the two tracks, Stroebe and Schut (1999) showed us that in order to deal with the great emotions of grief, we must oscillate between the past and the future but also between feeling the pain of grief and avoiding it.

This chapter is about the emotional dimension of the IPM and the big question: What can I do?

A hundred words for grief

The emotional dimension of grief counts many different emotions—despair, anxiety, guilt, anger, hostility, yearning, and longing. Traditionally, the emotional dimension of grief is well researched, and the emotional aspects of grief are therefore very clear and in the foreground for most people. Indeed, originally, grief itself was even considered to be a feeling or an emotional reaction that one had to "work through" (Bowlby, 1980; Freud, 1917/1957; Lindemann, 1944; Worden, 1991). Later, grief was perceived as a series of emotional stages with associated tasks.

Yet grief is not a passive state of emotion that we have to deal with.

In fact, we are very active as the grief unfolds, and one could therefore say that the grieving process is rather a complex interplay between our grieving activities and the emotional reactions we ourselves help to create. This means that we ourselves find different ways to express our grief: we talk to others about the loss and find ways to create emotional presence with others, we make up memorial rituals, we find ways to remember certain events in the past, and gradually, we find out how much we need to talk about our loss and grief in social contexts and who we need to talk to in order for it to help us. This means that we are very active in finding ways to be in touch with the loss and work to integrate it into our minds and emotions.

Philosopher Michael Cholbi from the University of Edinburgh published a book in 2021 called *A Philosophical Guide to Grief.* He points out that loss is indeed something that happens to us and that grief is inevitable, but most importantly:

"Grief is not just something that happens to us, grief is also something we do."

Cholbi (2022)

Although it is a complex interplay, the emotions of grief will shape our choices and actions, and at the same time, our choices and actions also shape our emotions. This explains why grief processes are so dynamic and have very individual courses. Another way of saying this is that as long as the grieving process is dynamic and life-changing, we are working to live with the loss, whereas when there is no dynamic interaction between feelings and actions, grief no longer is dynamic. Now, the process slows down, there is no movement toward an integration of the loss into life, and it may even stall and become completely stuck.

Text box 4.1   The grief orchestra

Imagine an orchestra as a metaphor for emotions. In the orchestra, different instruments play together to form a melody. Each instrument plays an important role in the total harmony of the music. The same can be said about the emotions of grief. In this orchestra, it is sadness, anger, and blame that play the various horns, while love, vulnerability, and gratitude play the harp and strings. Each emotion plays an important role in the overall melody, but when the horns play loudly, they are so intense and overwhelming that they overshadow the fine and delicate melody of the harp and strings.

Just as it can be difficult to hear the melody when some instruments are too loud, in the same way, it can be difficult to understand all aspects of grief when certain emotions are too intense. When this happens, feelings of anger, blame, and guilt can drown out feelings of love, relief, and pride. Now, there is a risk that we behave as if the overwhelming emotions make up the whole soundscape. While this is completely understandable, when we get caught up in the negative emotions of grief, we miss out on seeing the love, appreciation, admiration, and gratitude that are also important parts of grief. Now, the emotional expression of grief can become completely distorted because only certain emotions are communicated, and we end up feeling that others do not understand our grief because they do not hear all the expressions of it. The feelings that do not find a good expression keep on making noise in us until they are also heard and acknowledged.

The myth that feelings tell the truth

It is a popular myth that if we listen to our feelings, they will tell us the unconditional truth. But is that really so? We become aware of our emotions many times during a day, and here, our emotions are a source of information for us. They try to tell us something important and even motivate us to act. Contrary to popular belief, emotions do not contain an objective truth but rather are an expression of how our body reads, interprets, and reacts to the world.

As with the myth of true feelings, there are also myriad of popular beliefs about grief and living with loss. One of the most popular myths is that grief is best managed by doing emotional "grief work." In that understanding, it is best to express or vent emotions when grieving. Another myth is that if emotions contain basic truths, we should not try to change or work with the emotions we experience in grief. Instead, we must seek to gain insight into them. Some of these ideas were put forward by Freud in 1917 in his highly influential work *Mourning and Melancholia* (1917/1957). Here, Freud was exclusively aware of grief processes after the loss of a close person. As a psychiatrist, Freud helped his patients by using the "conversation cure" and listening to them talk about their innermost thoughts and conflicts. Although not described precisely, one can wonder how many of Freud's patients actually had various types of losses and suffered under them, as in the example that follows.

One of Freud's most famous case analyses is Anna O. (Breuer & Freud, 1895). In reality, her name was Bertha Pappenheim, and she was born in Vienna, Austria. Anna O. lost her sister to tuberculosis when Anna was just eight years old, and while she was a young woman, her father also contracted tuberculosis. Anna devoted herself to caring for her father, but his illness proved fatal. After this, Anna began to exhibit bizarre symptoms and was diagnosed with hysteria. She went through the talk therapy and got better. Since Anna was considered to be suffering from what was then called hysteria, there is in fact no description of her also talking about her losses and her grief. Nevertheless, Freud subsequently published his ideas about grief, which have later been called the grief work hypothesis.

Freud was a firm supporter of the idea: "You have to do your grief work." In a Freudian sense, this meant talking about the grief and working emotionally with the attachment to the deceased person, expressing the feelings related to that attachment in order to let go of the emotional bond. Freud called it catharsis (literally: purging or cleansing), when emotions were expressed in order to then release them. This would then also enable the bereaved to relinquish the emotional bond with the deceased person and attach themselves to new love objects. In 1920, however, it so happened that Freud himself lost his beloved daughter, Sophie, during the Spanish flu, and then he wrote to his friend Ludwig Binsvanger:

We know the pain we feel after a loss will continue;
it will also remain inconsolable, and we will never find a replacement.
No matter what we do, the pain is always there.
That's the way it should be.
It's the only way to perpetuate a love we don't want to give up.
(Freud, 1929)

Hence, Freud revised his own grief work hypothesis, at least unofficially. But the idea of letting go of the deceased has lived on in many models of loss since his time. Fortunately, since then, there has been quite a bit of research to increase our understanding of grief.

The question of whether the raw and painful emotions we experience in grief must be expressed in order for us to deal with them is much debated. In many Western countries, it is a popular idea that grief must be expressed in order to be healthy, and expressing the feelings will help the grief process along. This question has also been addressed via research, and here, it has been proven that the emotions of grief can overwhelm us with anger, remorse, shame, and guilt to such an extent that they leave us completely overwhelmed and numb. The American psychiatrist James Pennebaker has researched emotional expression and has stated that expressing emotions seems to be useful in terms of putting chaotic thoughts in their place so that we can find an appropriate response to them as well as helping us to accept what has happened (Pennebaker et al., 2001).

But when the emotional expression continues without limits,
then it seems to work in reverse.
You can compare it to throwing wood on a flaming fire,
the emotions flare up and grow bigger.

In this state, we can feel completely overwhelmed, and it is difficult to take responsibility for our process of grieving. The emotional discharge will continue without a natural end or also without it helping the person. It even seems that instead of talking ourselves out of the grief, we can talk ourselves into more grief.

It makes sense,
that it does not help us to confront the strong emotions
to do emotional processing
if we have not first built up an emotional tolerance for the strong emotions.

This means that we need more time or support to build up emotional tolerance, and patience and compassion are needed. But it also means that now, we are set to work on finding a way to build up this tolerance so that we can take responsibility for our way of grieving so that we do not become passive recipients of our feelings.

Living the question: What can I do?

In the IPM, the emotional dimension includes the emotional expressions of grief. When we are faced with a loss, it is natural to ask ourselves the question: What can I do in this situation? Therefore, this dimension in the IPM is linked with the ultimate existential question of freedom and how we can take responsibility for the situation. One of the aspects of grief that we often want to be able to do something about and take responsibility for is the strong emotions of grief.

At Columbia University in New York, the American psychologist George Bonanno and his colleagues, in their emotion laboratory, have studied grief and how we regulate emotional expressions when we experience loss. Mai-Britt visited them once and spoke to them about their nuanced studies of the severity and duration of grief. Bonanno calls it emotional flexibility when we have the ability to regulate emotions in a way that fits the context. This is done by reading the situation, making an assessment about whether our emotional response is useful, and if this is not the case, then adapting our response to match the environment (Bonanno et al., 2011). According to Bonanno, his studies suggest that we possess the capacity for emotional flexibility. In 2014, another American psychologist, James Gross, described much the same process and called it emotion regulation (Gross, 2014). He described it as the ability to regulate emotional states up and down by using different methods to divert our attention and using focus shifts and reframing our thinking, thereby changing our emotional response.

"Emotional regulation means both being able to process deep emotions,
but also to push emotions aside or minimize them to avoid being emotionally overwhelmed." (Bonanno & Burton, 2013)

To be clear, Gross is not talking about simply downplaying sad or negative feelings in order to hide them away or avoid them. If we stick to the image of an emotional grief orchestra, then Gross is rather talking about being the conductor of our own emotional orchestra. Studies on grief and emotion regulation point out:

It is just as relevant to be able to express feelings
As it is to be able to change them or reformulate them.
We can work on our emotional reactions
to learn healthier emotional patterns,
which can help us in a time of grief.

So while we cannot exactly create emotions at will, we are not completely passive recipients of emotions either. In one of the first studies by Gündel and colleagues, brains were scanned during a grief process, contributing to increasing our knowledge of grief by imaging the brain's work (Gündel et al., 2003). This neuropsychological study shows us that during the grief process, we activate a wide range of neural pathways that define and modulate our grief. The brain regulates the autonomic nervous system, draws on our episodic memory, retrieves concrete visual images and memories, and performs complex emotion management as well as mentalizing and coordinating all these functions. All this complex neural activity shows why grief is so unique and subjective. The study also provides new clues to understanding the complexity of grief as well as the neurobiological and health consequences of grief. Later studies have also tried to understand the neural basis for processing strong emotions and what happens when we feel overwhelmed by them or avoid them and try to regulate them (O'Connor, 2019). Such studies have helped us understand how emotion regulation may be a key aspect of grief processing.

In the IPM, emotion regulation is about allowing the emotions and being aware of them by giving them a name and accepting their presence. In this way, we can be curious about what they tell us but also let them come and go as emotions tend to do without attributing too much importance to them.

> In the IPM, emotion regulation is described
> as being able to be in touch with our grief
> even when it is very painful
> but also being able to minimize or push emotions aside
> when they become destructive.

Emotion regulation helps us to have more freedom to shape our own lives without the emotion processing becoming overwhelming to us. In the IPM, emotion regulation can help us while we are grieving so that we avoid that our emotions completely take over. In the IPM, emotion regulation is therefore considered a central strategy to be able to navigate the emotions of grief.

An image of emotion regulation in the IPM is illustrated by Rembrandt's beautiful painting of a ship at sea. Rembrandt painted *The Storm on the Sea of Galilee* in 1633 and shows us how a ship struggles in the storm as it is tossed to and fro by the great waves, the sails torn apart and waves crashing over its prow. In the corner of the painting, Rembrandt is seen together with Jesus in the ship as they try to calm the waves and save the lives of the 14 men on board the vessel. The painting here illustrates that we cannot fight against the strong forces of grief. As the waves of grief create emotional turmoil, it can feel as if we are at the mercy of the storms of our emotional life. But like Jesus and Rembrandt, we must let ourselves be carried while we calm the waves and navigate the storm by our attitude. When the waves become too high and turbulent, they can endanger the ship. What we can do ourselves is to accept the turmoil of the waves, because we cannot do anything about the storm itself. On the other hand, we can try to navigate the ship by controlling the sails. If the storm of grief is very strong and the emotional waves toss the ship from side to side, it is important to lower the sails so that the ship stays afloat. At these moments, we cannot expect any progress on our journey; the priority is to survive. Other days, the sea is calmer and the ship is able to move forward at a faster speed.

Emotion regulation is really about being able to identify the storms of grief and becoming aware of our emotions and getting to know the ups and downs.

This awareness can help us build emotional tolerance. It also means that we work to stay in touch with our own strengths and power despite grief putting pressure on our thinking and freedom of spirit. There is a big difference between wanting to avoid sadness or taking a break from sadness. The first is about the whole approach to grief, while the second is about temporarily diverting one's thoughts or focusing on something other than grief in order to better navigate the process. One way to start this process is to look for a balance between being in touch with the difficult feelings of grief and being in touch with life and something that also brings joy and quality of life.

The tension between doing and being

When the grieving process is defined by how we do grief and how we act in our grief, the emotional dimension in the IPM is characterized by the freedom we have to take responsibility or make our own choices in grief. That side of our grieving process is often not mentioned so much. Previous models of grief most often refer to grief as something we are subjected to. For existentialist thinkers like Frankl and Yalom, the ultimate concern of freedom and responsibility is defined by our absolute freedom to choose how to respond to adversity in our lives. The popular French philosopher and writer Jean-Paul Sartre had an even more extreme view of what it means to be human. He pointed out that we all struggle with the meaninglessness of life, but we possess the freedom to make choices about many crucial things in our lives, such as how we deal with loss and suffering. Sartre would argue that a person in a wheelchair perhaps does not have the same freedom of mobility as someone who is able to walk, but they can be called free because they have the freedom to choose how to interpret and understand their own existence. For Sartre, this is the ultimate aspect of existence (Sartre, 1943/2014). We all struggle to take responsibility and make choices about our lives, especially when faced with difficult life experiences. Here, it is easy to fail to see ourselves as responsible for our own existence and to excuse ourselves by thinking that we did not choose this fate, and therefore, it is not our fault, and hence, we cannot take responsibility for it. But Sartre would say that we always have a choice. If we do not take responsibility for our lives and our choices even in difficult situations, we will experience anxiety and a lack of authenticity (Sartre, 1943/2014). This is also the case when we experience loss.

It is when we do not take responsibility for our reactions and our future that we become particularly unhappy with our losses.

In grief, we struggle with the balance between using the emotions for information and giving them an expression. At the same time, we stabilize and minimize the emotions in order to find a way to live life without the emotions of grief overpowering us.

This can also be expressed as the tension between *doing* and *being*. Until the 18th century, the term used for emotions was *passiones animae* or passions of the soul (Dixon, 2012). The concept of "passion" in Latin is still very much alive in many languages. In English, we use it in words like *passion* and *passive* but also when we talk about one of the great pieces of music in Western European history, Bach's *St Matthew Passion*. What unites all these meanings related to the concept of *passio* is that they all refer to being affected by going through something: we can be affected by a great feeling of love and desire (passion), but we can also be affected by a feeling of pain and injustice, which we must find mainly a way of carrying rather than being able to act on it (passive).

This reveals something interesting from an existential perspective. It takes courage or strength to allow oneself to be in or feel the painful grief, as it exposes our vulnerability. In the grieving process, it means daring to be open to what we can call the passions of the soul, finding the inner courage to indulge in the feelings, but also to have contact with our power of action so that we can take responsibility for changing any feelings that do not help us into a deeper connection with ourselves and reality.

> The tension between being in grief and acting in grief
> gives room to take responsibility for the process
> by both being patient and embracing the grief
> but also responding and using one's strengths to act on the grief.

It may sound complex, but in everyday life, it means that we take turns to patiently let the grief have some space and to take responsibility and act on the grief.

This field of tension has become an important part of the IPM, as many of the studies on grief have shown the benefits of both taking time for grieving activities and taking time off from grief to take good care of oneself or take care of everyday functioning (Iglewicz et al., 2020; Stroebe & Schut, 1999). It makes sense that we need to be in touch with our grief, take time out for it, and do mourning activities, e.g., remembering, looking at pictures, going to the cemetery, etc. It seems that we also help ourselves by acting on other aspects of life and ensuring daily life, for example, cooking wholesome meals, going to the bank, talking to the insurance company, etc. Our emotions are useful tools in grief because they help us into awareness of what is happening and reveal our reactions to it, and they help us to process and integrate the loss into our understanding of the world. But the emotions are not so helpful when they overwhelm us and create a destructive state in us in which we cannot act or integrate the loss into our understanding of life. It is therefore a big task in grief to become aware of our feelings and assign them a rightful place in the grieving process.

The IPM points out the challenge between
finding a balance between being in grief and doing (acting on) grief.
We find the balance by using the indicator of
whether we are able to be connected to ourselves and our life force
while we are in grief.

Therefore, working on taking responsibility for our process in grief can be considered an act of love for ourselves and the people around us.

Our emotions are always in motion and change from one minute to the next, as the *motion* part of the word emotion indicates. It is also not uncommon to feel more than one emotion at a time, merging into a very complex emotional state within us. If we attach too much importance or power to all of our feelings, they can create a sense of instability or large fluctuations in our sense of self. If we do not actively work to become aware of our emotions, they will toss us around like a kite in a storm or like the ship in Rembrandt's painting. In fact, emotions can even make the grief process much more difficult if they spin out of control and start working against us because we become overwhelmed by them, or a few emotions drown out the whole emotional landscape, and now, we are no longer in touch with our grief but only with, for instance, anger or despair.

Naturally, it is relevant to have many different emotions when we are grieving. However, if you think about it, there are neither good nor bad feelings. Emotions inform us about the situation we are in and are a valuable source of information for us, whether it means being happy or sad. All emotions can be appropriate at different times, and they are all trying to tell us something that can help us navigate our lives. Therefore, emotions such as despair and sadness are not only negative, they are essential to inform us about the situation or our own state of being. It is when we are not aware of all the different emotions of grief that we can get lost in the grief process. The point is that we can only live with our grief when we are aware of all the different emotions we have inside us in grief.

Text box 4.2   Existential reflection—what role do emotions play in your life?

- How are you affected by your loss?
- How do you experience your grief? What emotions do you experience in your grief?
- What role do emotions play in your life? Are you used to listening to them and assigning them a specific role? Or are they just distractions to you?

- What do you do when you experience emotional pain? Are you trying to avoid it? Or do you think it is important to feel it or even express it?
- Are you aware of listening to all your different emotions in grief? Or are there certain feelings that you are not paying attention to?
- What emotions do you think are natural in grief? Can you express strong emotions in grief? How long can one express feelings in grief?
- How can you coexist with your grief?

Random acts of kindness and self-compassion

When we feel helpless, the best cure is, of course, to experience helpfulness. We tend to think that helpfulness must come from others for it to be soothing, but actually, helping ourselves or helping others also alleviates our own helplessness. There is a well-known poem called "Epitaph" by Merrit Malloy that is used in the Reform Jewish liturgy as an optional reading before the prayer Kaddish. In the poem, she expresses the wish that we use our sorrow and what we received from the person who died to do good things to other people. The same love we cannot give to the one who has left us can be given to the people around us who might also be in need of love and kindness (Malloy, 1988).

This poem has been used to show the value of random acts of kindness when we are grieving. A random act of kindness is, for example, leaving a loving note for a friend, praising a single parent, helping an elderly neighbor, giving flowers to a new colleague, baking a cake for coworkers, passing on a book that you have read, leaving your newspaper for someone else on the park bench, etc. The term "random acts of kindness" comes from a 2019 study by Lee Rowland and Oliver Scott Curry, who examined the impact of small acts of kindness. Here, it turned out that the small random acts of kindness spread like ripples in water: when you do it yourself, you will want to do it more often. When it's done for you, you'll want to pass it on. When you see it, you want to join in (Rowland & Curry, 2019). This shows us the power of kindness and compassion.

When we suffer, while we grieve, we are probably very used to thinking that we need understanding, compassion, and reassurance. It gives us a support that is soothing and that helps us calm the nervous system, all of which also stabilizes our emotional reactions.

We are probably used to thinking that support must be provided by others.
And while this can be a great help,
there is also another very central part of compassion and helpfulness:
The grieving persons themselves! This is called self-compassion or self-care.

The great thing about self-compassion is that it is always available, and it has been shown to be very effective. Self-compassion is a useful quality for dealing with our emotional imbalances, helping us navigate and balance grief. And we can actually train our self-compassion and use it to help other people when we want to support them in their loss and grief.

Self-compassion was introduced in 2003 by the psychologist Kirstin Neff as a way to develop a helpful attitude toward oneself. Originally derived from Buddhist psychology, self-compassion distinguishes three fundamental components that are mutually reinforcing: mindfulness, self-care, and shared humanity (Neff, 2003). All three elements are included in different dimensions of the IPM.

Text box 4.3   Three fundamental components of self-compassion

- Awareness: helps to get to know our grief and sets us free to choose how we want to grieve
- Self-care: regulates or balances feelings of grief so that we are not overwhelmed
- Shared humanity: protects us from isolation and unites us as humans in grief

---

Awareness refers to the ability to stay in the moment, to be aware of the thoughts and feelings that rise and fall without having to react on them or slip into rumination. This awareness is the balanced and non-judgmental awareness of our feelings and thoughts, which is also known as mindfulness. This is described in the IPM in the cognitive dimension (Chapter 5). In the IPM, it is described how, with the help of attention, we can get to know our grief and be aware of its fluctuations and pain. This type of awareness can offer a kind of freedom to understand and know grief and increase our tolerance but also set us free to make choices about how we want to grieve.

Self-care refers to looking at oneself in a kind and understanding manner, even if we are not always the best version of ourselves, as well as performing acts of self-love to do something good for ourselves. This is an important quality, as loss and grief can prompt us to ruminate on things we should have done differently in the past. If we do not practice self-care and self-compassion, then the self-criticism and our own condemnation can close us off from reality, and we now only see the negative distorted image. Self-care is not self-pity or self-absorption but acknowledging our own feelings without judgment, accepting the mistakes we may make with an understanding that no one is perfect, and looking with gentle eyes on our sufferings and failures because all humans experience adversity (Neff, 2011). In the IPM, self-care is described as a point of orientation in the emotional dimension, because the feelings of grief can be regulated or balanced by giving oneself care so that we are not so overwhelmed by the intense feelings of grief.

Last but not least, it is helpful to be able to see loss and grief as part of our common human experience of suffering. It has been shown to be helpful to be able to realize that we all suffer many losses during a lifetime and that it is part of being human that we can lose what we love or something that is important to us (Guldin, 2019). This is explained in the IPM's social dimension of isolation and connectedness (Chapter 6). If we believe that our loss happens because we are personally persecuted or condemned, the pain becomes much worse. The IPM suggests instead that the pain must be balanced with all the love and appreciation that we have also found in life. The more we can find a connectedness in feeling part of humanity or a community, a group or a family that has this loss in common, the less isolation we will feel. Loss and grief unite us as humans rather than divide us. This attention can counter the experience of loss and grief as separating and isolating, ending in a painful loneliness.

The better we can cultivate an attitude of self-compassion while grieving, the more we will be able to find a way to balance and regulate the difficult reactions of grief. Self-compassion can increase our sense of connectedness with ourselves, our ability to carry our grief and provide us with more personal strength.

Text box 4.4   Existential reflection—which actions help you in grief

- What strengths do you have that can help you in your grief?
- What helps you to be connected to yourself in your grief?
- What can help you find good grounding when you experience intense emotions?
- Are there specific grieving activities that help you get in touch with your grief? For example, meditation, grief diary, letter writing, memorial rituals, or something else?
- How do you "do" your grief and take responsibility for it?
- How can self-care help you alleviate your suffering? For example, yoga, exercise, nature, walks, gardening, prayer, etc.
- Can reading poetry or literature help you to be in touch with your grief? Listening to music?

The transformative potential of emotional regulation

Grief means
"to descend into the abyss of our existence
to return to the surface of our being."
(van Deurzen, 2023)

The well-known existential psychologist Emmy van Deurzen has said about working with grieving persons that "the work is always focusing on life's pain, being willing to explore the darkest sides of being without being destroyed by our experiences" (van Deurzen, 2023). Existential therapists view freedom and responsibility as ultimate existential balances we all must deal with. We may think that freedom is good and pleasant, but in an existential understanding, there is always a necessity with freedom, namely having to navigate, take responsibility, and make choices. Emmy van Deurzen explains that as a therapist, she would start by looking at how the world of the bereaved has changed and then how the person is affected by it. She would also talk to the bereaved about understanding that this emotional state is natural, and although painful, it is also part of the full experience of life that we will have to accept as part of a normal life.

Yalom wrote that he talked to his patients about taking responsibility for their grief. He writes in his book on existential therapy that one of the things that affects our mental health the most is that we avoid taking responsibility. He is convinced that especially in the face of existential difficulties, personal freedom and responsibility are particularly important (Yalom, 1980).

> When we face grief, we cannot change what we have lost,
> but we can take responsibility for the grief we experience.

It is a basic existentialist thought that even if it feels meaningless, we have no other options than to look for meaning in what cannot be changed. Then we are back at the Serenity Prayer in the beginning of this chapter, which just pointed out that we must dare to accept what we cannot change. It takes a lot of courage, but if we refuse responsibility for our grief, the emotions will ultimately rule over us and our situation.

The American psychiatrist John Schneider described in his book *The Overdiagnosis of Depression. Recognizing Grief and Its Transformative Potential* the idea that grief holds a potential for self-development and transformation for the griever (Schneider, 2000). Schneider explains that the pain of grief is a source of change if we can let the grief develop without trying to avoid it (Guldin, 2019). If we have the strength to regulate our grief and give it the opportunity to unfold naturally, grief also has the potential to show us new insights and help us search for new meaning and hope.

How are we to understand these psychologists and psychiatrists? In the IPM, grief is described as a balance in which we must learn to navigate and balance our grief.

> We look for ways to "do" our grief—take responsibility for it and make choices—
> but also to "be" in our grief, giving it space, feeling it, and trying to learn from it.

In other words, we must live the question, as Rilke wrote (Rilke, 2000), about how we want to regulate emotions. It is an answer we live into, and not one that can be given once and for all.

This chapter has discussed why grief is described by some as a stress reaction with large emotional fluctuations. Although we tend to think that stress and intense emotions are dangerous, studies have shown that the very same forces in our minds also have the potential to reorganize our thinking and move us out of habitual thought patterns. It forces us to discover new content in life. Therefore, this chapter describes the emotional struggles of grief and which frames of mind we can look for as points of orientation in grief. If we misunderstand our emotions or do not see them for what they are—informative biochemical movements in our body—then we can end up giving our emotions too much power. In this regard, the IPM suggests navigating the emotions by doing emotion regulation. This means that sometimes, we focus on giving room for and following the feelings of grief, and at other times, focus is on taking responsibility for the grief, regulating it by practicing self-care, or even distracting ourselves from the intense feelings because they no longer help us into connectedness with the grief.

> When we let grief unfold, grief has the potential
> to lead us to some of our existential points of development,
> for example, can I ask for help? or do I have the courage to show my
>   vulnerability?

For most people, it is also a point of development to deal with the intense feelings of grief without letting them overwhelm us or to avoid them or fight them so much that they create chaos inside us. If we do not try to face this challenge, we can reduce our tolerance for the existential suffering life presents and then run into bigger challenges later, because now we become anxious every time life challenges us.

Grief is sometimes defined as our natural way of healing after a loss. Let us assume for a moment that grief comes with a natural desire to take us to a new place where we can contain the grief. This means that grief opens up new depths in the mind and invites reflection and contemplation. For a while, all energy is turned inward.

> If we can face the painful emotional states we encounter in grief,
> it is likely that this can lead us on the way to
> an increased sense of freedom and a new openness toward a greater perspec-
>   tive on life,
> because now, we can accept all aspects of life, both the joyful and the painful.

In grief, we struggle because we have to give up something, which gives us a deep sense of powerlessness, but if we dare to look at this powerlessness, it also comes with a sense of liberation. It frees us from the urge to take responsibility for losses over which we have no control. The pain is already within us, and the question is whether we look at it or not. It is a common misconception that we increase the pain if we give it space. But the pain is already there. Grieving people tell us that by paying attention to their grief, they have expanded their emotional register and experience more intense emotions. Sometimes, powerlessness or meaninglessness are the most dominant feelings, but at the same time, there is a deeper sense of appreciation of life, of meaning in existing, and even more intense love as it has become clear that we cannot take it for granted. There is also an increased sense of vulnerability that must be seen in the light of an increased sensitivity to what life has to offer and the sensitivity to appreciate the beauty in the smallest thing.

Central points in Chapter 4

- The emotional dimension in the IPM is about the broad spectrum of emotions in grief.
- It is a normal reaction to want to run away from the pain of grief.
- Contrary to popular belief, emotions do not contain an objective truth but rather are an expression of how our body reads, interprets, and reacts to the world.
- Expressing feelings can be helpful, but when emotional outpouring is not controlled, it can emotionally overwhelm us and make the pain worse.
- Grief is both something we do and something that happens to us. "Doing" and "being" in grief are brought together in a higher unity in emotion regulation, which requires both action and patience.
- The emotional dimension in the IPM is characterized by the existential balance between freedom and responsibility.
- In our quest to use our freedom and take responsibility for our lives, we navigate between doing and being.
- Compassion is not just a matter of receiving something from others; it can be just as helpful to practice self-compassion and self-care or to spread small acts of kindness toward others. The beneficial effects are remarkable.
- Grief has the potential to transform us. If we can let grief unfold, it has the potential to give us new insight, meaning, and hope.
- If we can face the painful emotional states of grief, it is likely that they can lead us on the path to a sense of new openness and inner freedom, which can give us a greater perspective on life, because we have now learned to accept all aspects of life, both the joyful and the painful events.

Interlude: Ann's struggle with the emotional dimension of the loss

Ann gradually felt her energy return and her appetite improved, now she could relax again, read a book, and go for a walk. However, she became increasingly irritated by the loss of control over her body, the mood swings, the sleep disturbance, and sometimes even emotional outbursts. She felt herself questioning many aspects of her life, feeling a deep sadness about her parents' troubles, a lot of anger toward her aunt, and even toward this former boyfriend who had not tried to understand her choices. She did not know what to do with all these emotions, and she felt a kind of alienation from herself, like she was no longer quite herself. She felt that her personal freedom was significantly curtailed.

Ann was used to taking the initiative and being proactive in improving her quality of life, so she talked to her GP about the symptoms. They had a talk about well-being and menopause, and the doctor initially suggested that she try herbal medicine, which might be able to reduce the symptoms, before possibly starting a hormone treatment. One of her girlfriends had also advised her to start yoga so that her body could find new well-being.

One of the following evenings, Ann sat and had a glass of wine while watching TV. She stumbled upon a documentary about adopted children. Some of the children struggled with feelings of being unwanted or even homeless, and this gave them a sense that they could not fully understand their own identity. The documentary affected Ann a lot and rekindled memories of growing up with her aunt. When she went to bed, she felt a deep sadness and loneliness, and in the days that followed, the documentary kept working in the back of her mind. She could not help thinking that all her life, she had thought she had great freedom and that her work, her career, and her lifestyle had given her the feeling of being free. But now, she began to doubt whether these were really free choices. Because underneath all the comfort, she could sense that it had also been about finding a place in life and a struggle to feel at home. She was a little confused and even felt a little anxious to discover that all her financial and job-related freedom might have also been about an emotional lack of freedom.

In the Center for Grief and Existential Values, we suggested that Ann reflect on how she, on an existential level, had struggled to find meaning or a framework for her life. When you experience loss, it is not uncommon to doubt that your choices were the right ones. It seemed that her choices gave her the feeling of being "at home" in her life; however, she now pondered whether they also gave her the feeling of having avoided something. This seemed like an important discovery to start regulating the emotional work and finding a new balance between feeling freedom and taking responsibility.

Chapter 5

The cognitive dimension. What have I lost?

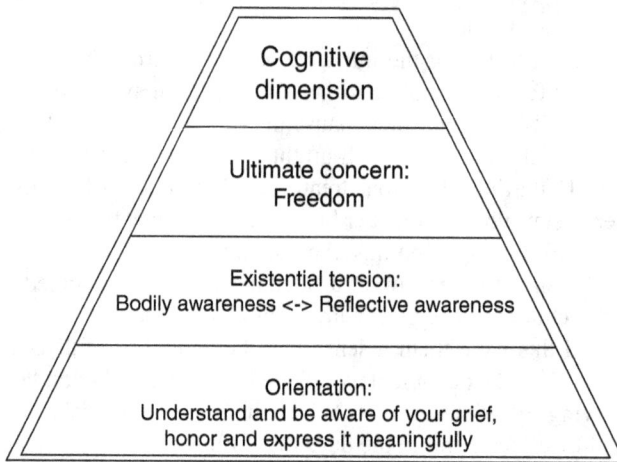

Figure 5.1 The cognitive dimension of the IPM depicted as the segment of a pentagon containing the ultimate concern of freedom, the existential tension between bodily awareness and reflective awareness, and some directions.

"Finding the center of strength within ourselves is in the long run the best contribution we can make to our fellow men. . . . One person with indigenous inner strength exercises a great calming effect on panic among people around him. This is what our society needs—not new ideas and inventions; important as these are, and not geniuses and supermen, but persons who can 'be,' that is, persons who have a center of strength within themselves."

(May, 1953)

Magical thinking

Joan Didion, the famous American author, tells us in her book *The Year of Magical Thinking*, the story of her own magical thinking after the loss of her husband,

DOI: 10.4324/9781003499060-5

John Dunne (Didion, 2005). In 2003, Dunne died very suddenly of a heart attack in their home while sitting down to eat dinner. In the year that passed after her loss, Didion tried to make sense of the end of their symbiotic partnership, her mind revolving around the magical thought that John would return. In her mind, she relives and analyzes her husband's death, focusing with each repetition in her mind different emotional and physical aspects of the death. Gradually, she accepts the loss and integrates the experience into her thoughts, after which it becomes clear to her how much energy she has spent on these magical thoughts (Didion, 2005).

The concept of magical thinking has been introduced in both anthropology and psychology and captures the idea that we can become convinced that we can change the world with our thoughts, wishes, or rituals. For example, if we hope for it intensely, then an inevitable event can be averted. Or if we knock on wood, a wish comes true. In the book, Didion is haunted by questions about the medical details of Dunne's death, whether he in advance sensed and gave her signals that he was going to die. She tries to change the course of events by giving new meaning in her mind to the actions and conversations that took place before his death.

Didion is no exception. As we grieve, we struggle to accept the reality of loss and understand death, absence, and emptiness. Along the way, we do a lot of somersaults in our minds as we interpret the world in an idiosyncratic way, trying to make sense of our altered reality and assigning personal meaning to what has happened.

Although it may sound a little crazy, magical thinking is quite common when we are grieving. We continuously interpret our experiences and strive to find meaning in what happens. This is also called meaning construction. When we face loss, we question the meaning, and even though the loss will probably never make sense, we still look for a meaning in what happened, or we try to fit the loss into the beliefs we already have about life. For example, if we are already convinced that we are unlucky in life, then we will interpret our losses in light of this. We attach meaning based on the schemas we already have in our minds, and only after a long struggle will we realize that we may have to incorporate a new understanding of the world to integrate the loss. For example: I did not lose my job because I am unlucky in life but because that function was closed down.

Robert Neimeyer, a psychology professor at the University of Memphis, has worked for years to describe the processes we go through to construct meaning when our understanding of the world has been challenged by a loss. He believes that grief involves the reaffirmation or reconstruction of the world and the meaning that has been challenged by the loss (Neimeyer, 2001). This is exactly what Didion tried to describe to us in her book on magical thinking. We are all trying to understand our loss and understand ourselves in the context of the loss. In the IPM, this is described as an existential opening, where we try to understand our whole existence in light of the loss.

This chapter describes the cognitive dimension in the integrative understanding of grief. That is, all the effects and expressions of grief in our mind and thought processes, as well as the big question of trying to understand "what have I lost?"

The cognitive expression of grief

Grief is a complex condition that includes many mental functions and affects our thinking. In addition to *magical thinking*, the cognitive aspects of grief include experiencing the situation as surreal, thinking counterfactually (against the facts), being preoccupied with thoughts of the loss, overthinking and brooding, and trying to make sense and find meaning in what has happened. At the same time, many of us experience problems with our concentration and memory and many other mental aspects of grief (Brennan & Dash, 2009; Neimeyer et al., 2021). Our cognitive processes are difficult to distinguish from the emotional and physiological processes already described (Chapters 3 and 4), but especially this tossing and turning of all aspects of the loss in our thoughts and the whole coordination of the different processes of grief is important to note when trying to characterize the cognitive expression of grief. We also use our consciousness to find meaning in the reactions we have after the loss, interpret the loss, and consider how we can best respond to the changed situation (Lazarus & Folkman, 1984; Stroebe & Schut, 1999). It also means that we think a lot about how we grieve, for example, whether our thoughts are relevant and appropriate. This is also called metacognition. We also consider how much we should talk to others about our grief, and we especially think a lot about why this happened to us and what exactly it means for us. This is also called attributing personal meaning or meaning construction. We might even read ourselves into the event, believing that we created the situation or can control uncontrollable events, and then we end up spending our time thinking about how we could have avoided the event. This is what Didion so masterfully reports about her own magical thoughts describing how she wished to have avoided her husband's death if only she had read the signs. Her thoughts also revolved around the idea that her husband knew what awaited him and tried to prepare her for it. Whether John Dunne knew he was about to die we cannot know, nor does the book reveal any convincing signs of it, but Didion shows us many aspects of what we call construction of meaning. In the IPM, this is called "living the question." It seems comforting to Didion—or perhaps to all of us—to think that her husband knew he was going to die soon and that he tried to protect her from this knowledge while lovingly preparing them both for it.

It shows us that grief cannot be understood without understanding the individual who is grieving.

Grief is deeply rooted in the griever's bodily senses,
emotional processing, thought patterns, experiences,
and even beliefs about life and the world.
This makes every grieving process individual and unique.

From this unique starting point, we try to make sense of what is happening. In this process, it becomes clear that we use our previous cognitive schemas to make sense of the loss, but if they don't work, then we have to build new understandings or new models of the world as we are grieving. Therefore, the cognitive dimension in the IPM is also about our personal freedom to understand our grief process and assign personal meaning to it. We usually ask ourselves the question "what have I lost" while our thoughts revolve around the loss and what we lost.

Grief as a learning process

In her 2022 book on the grieving brain, the American psychologist and neuroimmunologist Mary-Frances O'Connor hypothesizes that grief is a learning process for the brain (O'Connor, 2022). O'Connor's research is about losing a loved one, and she explains that the brain has difficulty understanding that the person we have lost, who constantly occupies our thoughts, is exactly the same person who is no longer here with us in real life. The person we long for and constantly think about and who evokes strong feelings in us is the same person who can no longer respond to these feelings. This discrepancy between thought and feeling processes and the lack of presence in reality ends up being a puzzle for our brain. Therefore, O'Connor describes it as a learning process for the brain to understand that the person is not alive or present in reality but only lives in our memory and in our emotions. Mary-Frances O'Connor uses the metaphor of phantom pain, which explains that when an arm or leg is removed, the nerve activity does not stop, so it takes a long time for the brain to understand that the arm or leg is no longer there. It takes time for the brain to change the neural pathways when a close person is no longer there or if they have changed due to illness and are no longer the same person. You could say that everything we care about is represented in the brain as a part of us, and it takes time to rewire the neural activity and understand the concept of loss, gone, and especially gone forever.

But what if the brain starts a learning process when we have lost a close person or something else we care about? It reminds us of a situation with one of the neighbor's children: a little boy who would sometimes come to our home when the children were little. If he stayed for dinner and he came across a new dish which was unknown or maybe strange to him, he would say: "I have not learned to eat that yet." Apart from being sweet, it was also clever, as with this phrase, no one could ever accuse him of being a picky eater. He simply explained that he was in a learning process, and everyone can respect that.

What if we could all claim a similar learning process when we grieve?
Then we could say: "I know I talk a lot about my loss,
but that is because my brain is still trying to understand
that he is no longer here with us."

We probably all recognize this type of learning process when trying to under-stand something painful in life. Grief is also a matter of changing our usual thought patterns. We may be familiar with the idea that grief can shut down our brain, but a new way of looking at it is that grief creates new pathways of thought and changes in our neural activity. It takes time, but this process opens our minds to new under-standings in life and transforms our outlook on life and our existential awareness. In Rilke's words (Rilke, 2000), this can also be called "living the question."

Where is our consciousness when we grieve?

Since the philosopher Immanuel Kant (1724–1804) published his work on human consciousness, most philosophers and psychologists would probably say that there is no such thing as an objective reality. The world is dependent on the mind that sees it. The eye *sees* only what *the mind* is prepared to understand.

One might even say that our experience of grief is dependent on the mind
  that sees.
If we have experienced many previous losses,
we may view our next loss differently
than if it is completely new to us that also we might lose someone or
  something.

Therefore, it may also seem strange that the study of human consciousness did not appeal very much to psychologists throughout most of the 20th century. Instead, for many years, the subject was treated in philosophy and especially within the dis-cipline of phenomenology by philosophers such as Edmund Husserl (1859–1938), Martin Heidegger (1889–1976), and Maurice Merleau-Ponty (1908–1961). The American psychologist and founder of existential therapy Rollo May, quoted in the beginning of the chapter, was also very interested in phenomenology. The most important object of study for phenomenology is the exploration of our conscious-ness but also how our mind is biased in experiencing reality. For the phenomenolo-gists, the ultimate source of all meaning and value is man's own lived experience. However, we must learn to understand our own biases if we want to come closer to understanding the world. Rollo May puts it this way: "Many people suffer from the fear of finding themselves alone, and then they don't find themselves at all" (May, 1953).

Maybe we can become so afraid of our own aloneness that we do not look
  for who we are at all.

In existential phenomenology, the emphasis is placed on the study of the world through the meaning we place on life. You could say that we impose meaning on the world all the time, and this means that every day, we are engaged in the study of *what is real*. We may just not consider it a philosophical process but rather a process based on cognition. We try to make sense of all our experiences through a mental process in which we perceive and sense or acquire knowledge through our experiences, and then our mental processes work to understand the world. For this cognitive process, we use our attention, processing, thinking, memory, imagining, reasoning, and even putting words to our experiences and communicating them to the outside world. Therefore, this cognitive process is also a large part of our grieving process.

Text box 5.1   Existential-phenomenological exercise

- Can I look at the meaninglessness of my loss with an open mind?
- How can I live the questions I have about my loss—rather than trying to make explanations?
- Can I refrain from constructing magical thoughts or causal explanations and look with openness at the loss I have suffered?
- Can I live with the open questions of the incomprehensibility of my loss?
- Can I live with open questions and be patient with myself and the world around me in relation to my loss?
- How can I allow myself to feel (the pain in) my body after the loss I have suffered?
- Are there words, poems, metaphors, symbols, songs, pictures, etc. that come to mind when I deal openly with my loss? Can they help me express my grief?

Living the question: What have I lost?

After a loss, understanding the loss and rebuilding meaning are cognitive processes.

The IPM illustrates that the emotional, social, and spiritual dimensions interact,
but it is our cognitive abilities that coordinate the process of exploring new sources of meaning, integrating the assumptions we already hold,
and through this process finding out what is it that I have lost,
what does it mean to me, and how can life make sense again.

Neurophysiological research confirms that during grief, our brain activates episodic memory (O'Connor, 2019). That is, we draw on our memory when we enjoy the good memories of, for instance, a deceased person or experiences we have had that are no longer here. While grieving, we deal with the memories of the lost person or object in our daydreams, preoccupied with thinking about what we lost and what it means to us now that it is gone.

> There is also a completely different layer in our thinking about grief.
> We also think about how to grieve.

This different layer is also called metacognition and means that we consider and reflect on the process we are going through and try to find out what is the best way to grieve and whether we should talk more with others or think less about the past, etc. (O'Connor, 2019). This also means that all the different cognitive processes can explain some of the differences between how each of us integrates the loss into our thinking and adapts to the loss or whether we end up suffering from the grief getting stuck somewhere in this process (O'Connor, 2019). The IPM therefore also points out that our attention and awareness become crucial in the integration of the loss and the transition to a different life. The point of the IPM is that we all use a phenomenological approach to our grief by allowing ourselves to look at it, pay attention to it, and hold it at arm's length, unfolding the experience and examining our grief.

> The IPM points out that we must let our strong mental powers work for us and make grief more conscious.

This means that we should not simply lean on the elaborated theories or models to understand our grief but rather use a phenomenological approach and our awareness to observe our own experience and our own reactions to loss. Only in this way can we become wiser about our own grief.

Text box 5.2   Reflection: observing our own thinking about loss

- How do you try to understand the loss you are experiencing?
- What understandings of life do you use? For example, that something is natural, unfair, meaningless, controllable, or other thoughts?

- Have you noticed if your losses require you to change your understanding of life? So what changes should you make?
- Do you have an assumption of how to grieve? What should grief look like?
- How is your grief affected by your outlook on life, loss, and grief? Does it make the grief harder or easier?
- Do you feel like your understanding of life and loss is changing/evolving to include your most recent loss?

Living loss

Grief does not wait until there is a death; grief starts the second we feel a loss in our lives. Many people, for example, live with what might be called "living loss" (Olshansky, 1962). Living loss is a theory of grief that emerged around the turn of the century. The term originally refers to the experience parents of a child with a disability may have and refers to the losses that chronic health problems or functional variations bring with them and the grief that follows. Living loss can also be experienced by people with dementia or other neurological disorders, cancer, heart or lung disease and by their families as they live with the losses that the disease has inflicted on them. This type of lasting grief is not a diagnosis and should not be confused with the ICD-11 diagnosis of *prolonged grief disorder*, which is a mental disorder developed by a small percentage of grievers and has been shown to be treatable with psychotherapeutic interventions. Living loss should also not be confused with the concept of *anticipatory grief*, which the psychiatrist Erich Lindemann coined in 1944 to describe the grief reaction of widows who expected to lose their husbands during the Second World War when they were drafted into the war (Lindemann, 1944) (see also p. 72). Living loss is not necessarily an expectation of death but rather that life is full of loss due to illness or events where our relationships and roles have to be rearranged, our futures changed, and our past dreams and visions die.

The living losses show us how loss and grief are natural parts of life: they make us aware of the limitations, vulnerability, and mortality of human existence. The IPM has included this in the understanding of grief and therefore points in the direction of this fundamental question: Who am I when I experience the losses that life inflicts on me, and how can I live my life with them?

The concept of living loss shows us that we mourn all our losses continuously, and this understanding is brought into the IPM.

From an existential perspective,
living loss also brings forth living grief,
which means that grief over a loss is activated again and again
as the understanding of loss and life evolves.

When we become more aware of the many different losses in our lives and the grief that follows us throughout our lives, we can also become more sensitive to life's many different losses.

The impossible question of meaning

Let us focus a little more on our reflective awareness of our grief and look at different ways our mind can work with grief. The German philosopher Wilhelm Dilthey (1833–1911) would say that there are two ways our thoughts can work: The first way he calls "explaining" (German: *erklären*) and the second way "understanding" (German: *verstehen*) (Dilthey, 1883). When we try to explain a situation, a feeling, or a condition, we look for causes. We create a logical chain of events that explains why something has happened so that we can make it understandable. Sometimes, it is helpful, for example, when we explain that it is not strange that we feel tired and lack appetite after we have suffered a great loss, because research has shown several aspects that can explain this. The body is full of adrenaline or stress hormones, and the alert response suppresses the feeling of hunger. In this case, rational knowledge helps us navigate the situation by explaining why we get tired and do not feel hungry. In this situation, it might be best to work on stress regulation, go for a walk in nature, and eat small, frequent meals.

Explaining and looking for causality is the way the natural sciences work. It is very important and useful in many situations. But explanations like these also have their limitations. If we lose a child to leukemia and ask ourselves, "Why did my child die?" it is not very helpful to hear that all people are mortal, leukemia is a potentially fatal disease, and statistically, our child was among the children who could not be saved. In this case, a causal explanation would completely fail to provide an answer to the "why" question that could help the person understand the loss. At first glance, the question "Why did my child die?" sounds like a question for a causal explanation (*explaining*), but it is probably rather a question that calls for finding meaning in the loss (*understanding*). The question is much more than just a question that calls for a clear answer or some information. The question: "Why did my child die?" can be reformulated into a statement: "This does not make sense. There is no horizon or frame of understanding that can make me understand the meaning of what has happened." Looking for meaning and connections between meanings is the way the humanities work. Our reflective consciousness looks both for causal explanations and for meaning structures. Both have their strengths and their limitations, and by combining them, we have the most comprehensive reflection. The combination of both natural sciences and humanities is exactly what the IPM aims for.

What we all share as humans when we experience loss and grief
can be expressed by finding causal relationships
using the language of "explaining."
But what is related to each person's experience of loss and grief

can only be expressed by finding unique structures of meaning in the individual's life
using the language of "understanding."

If we go back to the example of losing a child, how can we discover the existential meaning of the question "Why did my child die?" Understanding the existential significance of such an event is not like looking up the meaning of a word in a dictionary or the explanation of a disease online. Instead, it means that we enter into an existential process that can take time. Existential meaning is not found in fixed structures like causal relationships, but meaning develops in a dynamic process of living the question and gradually understanding it. Structures of meaning are part of the creative process of living and reflecting, and they can change at different times in life. When we read Dostoevsky at the age of 16, we will have a completely different understanding of the text compared to when we read the same book at the age of 56. The literal meaning of the words will be the same, but the same words in the book will resonate within us with new existential experiences, and the layers of meaning we use to find structures of meaning will be much more developed and complex.

Take the example of a young person trying to understand why she had to struggle with all the losses inflicted on her because she grew up with a mentally ill mother. In the beginning, she struggles to understand what it means to be mentally ill. Ten years later, the losses will have a completely different meaning and affect her identity development and basic security in life. Another ten years later, it will affect her parenting skills and opportunities in building her own family. However, in the long run, growing up with a mentally ill mother could contribute to developing a deeper existential view of life because she has had to deal with aspects of life, death, loneliness, and meaning from an early age. For this young woman, there is no complete understanding of the meaning of the mother's illness at any age but simply a continuous process of meaning construction. Still, this attribution of meaning is not just a process that takes place in our minds. Finding a deeper meaning is also about looking for it, being open to it, and becoming aware that life is speaking to me. It can also be Dostoevsky's book that speaks to me and will teach me something about my life that affects my existence and being in the world if I am open to it. Meaning we find, in love, connectedness, nature, literature, art, or music and many other places. However, to find it, we have to look for it and search for it in our own way.

Over time, most of us will also find
that although our loss causes a lot of grief and suffering,
it will also constitute a kind of opening to look for our own meaning in life.
It is when life speaks to us that we get a chance to experience what life is all about.

Developing a sensitivity to deeper meaning is a lifelong process shaped by existential experiences in our lives, those moments when life seems to be speaking to us in a way that is connected to the ultimate existential concerns of death, freedom, isolation, and meaninglessness. Loss and grief can be experienced as openings in which life speaks to us. In order to find a way to be in grief in the cognitive dimension, the IPM tries to point out that our reflective awareness is important and that we can use our reflections quite consciously to look for our attitude.

Text box 5.3 Existential reflection—the development of our understanding of loss

- Try to describe how you understood life, loss, and death as a 20-year-old.
- Then try to describe your understanding of life, loss, and death at your current age.
- What are the differences? What has changed?

Bodily awareness

Do you know the experience that we like certain images of another person because they give us a specific sensation or feeling of being in contact with that person? This sensation resides in our body. Hence, mindfulness and awareness are not just about our thoughts working to construct or assign meaning, as is often described in books about grief. There is also a body that sees the loss, hears the sound of it, and feels the grief (Merleau-Ponty, 1945). Our body has its own attention. It is with our bodies that we meet the world and communicate and interact with others.

Text box 5.4 Bodily reflection

- Try for a moment to think of a person, place, or value that you have lost. Focus on your memories of the person/place/value and situations you have enjoyed. Also consider what the person lost meant to you, how you experienced being with the person or being in that place, and what you learned from them.
- Now try to send your focus back to your own body and notice how your memories are stored as part of your bodily memory. How does it feel in your body when you think of this person/this place/this value?

All our memories resonate in our body and senses. The physical impact of the loss of someone we are connected to can be intense and overwhelming. We connect with others by integrating them into our senses and our bodies in ways that our thoughts or cognitive awareness alone cannot understand.

The existential psychotherapist and professor of psychology Ernesto Spinelli describes what he calls bodily phenomenology. Phenomenology has previously been explained as an important way of accessing our lived experience of grief. It is understood as the study of a phenomenon such as grief as it presents itself directly to us in a lived experience that has not yet been interpreted in the words and concepts that structure our thinking and speech. Bodily phenomenology indicates that we use the body as a way of experiencing the world directly, without all the preconceptions of thought and spoken words (Spinelli, 2015).

> Our bodies are carriers of our life history,
> our experiences, feelings, memories, and our whole brain.
> When we think about what we have lost, we delve into our memories
> or yearn for something we've lost.
> Then we use our body to get in touch with this memory.

Emotions can be easily read on our faces, in the way we carry ourselves, and in the way we move—especially for people who know us well. Anxiety is evident because we sweat and the heart beats strongly, and love is evident because of the warm, tingling feeling and the heart that skips a beat. This is also the case when we think about what we have lost. We can almost feel the other person or the lost next to us. Our body carries traces of the other person or object, and our memory is embedded in our whole body—not just our brain. Memory is therefore not only a mental task but also a felt sensation of what we have lost. This is sometimes referred to as bodily awareness. Consider, for example, how many paintings Picasso painted of Dora Maar, the many different ways he portrayed her, and the different situations we find her in in his pictures. Picasso's paintings are very sensual and abstract because he conveys a felt sense of Dora Maar.

In the IPM, the awareness of our bodily memory is integrated as an important part of our grieving process. It is based on research on bodily phenomenology, in which mind and body are not seen as being a dualistic relationship but as two sides of the same memory. It is because our body is the medium through which we access the world that we can say we exist and our body always experiences or "knows" more than our conscious mind. Our understanding and memories of what we have lost are bodily sensations as much as neurological memories.

> The IPM points out that we work with grief both in a bodily awareness and a cognitive awareness.

Consciousness is a tension between reflection and body

In the IPM, the cognitive dimension of grief is linked with the ultimate existential concerns about our freedom, because awareness can help us on the path to more inner freedom. But this freedom comes with a responsibility to make some choices. We can only do that if we are aware of both our reflective and bodily awareness. According to the Austrian psychiatrist Viktor Frankl, we always have freedom: In every situation, there is a moment, sometimes just a split second, between something that happens to us and our choice of response to the situation. This moment is the opening that enables me to give my personal response to something that happens to me (Frankl, 1946/2006). The freedom to choose my answer enables me in that moment to take responsibility and shape my life. We may come to believe that this moment is not there when there is loss, because grief is not experienced as a choice. But Frankl (1946/2006) and Yalom (1980) would say that this moment also exists when there is loss and grief.

> Every loss opens up the opportunity
> to reflect on my free response to what happens to me.

When we think about it, this means that the same cognitive skills that can help us distance ourselves from the situation and inform us about how the grieving process works also follow specific thought patterns that we are used to using to understand the world. So how do we know if our explanations are becoming self-referring and out of touch with reality? A reflective consciousness will ponder, rationalize, and "produce" meaning. The same applies to bodily awareness. The body has its own wisdom, and it keeps us grounded when our thoughts wander. But the pitfall can be that we overinterpret bodily sensations, pretending that the body speaks directly and unambiguously to us, that our feelings are always true, and that bodily signals are intuitions that hold a deeper truth.

Human beings are mind and body at the same time. But what is first and what is secondary? Are we primarily a body that is also thinking? Or are we primarily a mind or a soul that is embodied? Many philosophers, religious traditions, and scientists have tried to clarify the relation between these two dimensions of our humanity that are interrelated in such a mysterious way. Let us think about this mystery for a moment.

Text box 5.5   Existential reflection about the paradox of being human

- Look into the mirror and ask yourself: what am I as a human being?
- How does it feel if I consider myself as a biological entity, a mortal organism that is composed of materiality, a bunch of well-organized cells that

produces a kind of self-awareness and rational thinking as a byproduct of its biological functioning?

- How does it feel if I consider myself as a rational entity, a soul that is essentially eternal but temporarily embodied and mortal because of its biological basis?
- Which one of the two options is closest to how I feel?
- Do you think it is possible to reconcile both ways of looking at who we are?

In existentialist thinking, there is an agreement that being human means being unfinished and under construction. The reason for this is that as humans, we will never completely arrive at being who we are. The Danish philosopher Kierkegaard formulated this in the following way:

"Man is a synthesis of the infinite and the finite, of the temporal and the eternal, of freedom and necessity, in short it is a synthesis. A synthesis is a relation between two factors. So regarded, man is not yet a self."

(Kierkegaard, 1849/1941)

Kierkegaard formulated a very influential thought that would become the beginning of existentialist thinking: because humans are composed of opposites (mind and body, matter and spirit, freedom and necessity), we have a task of finding who we are, our authenticity, in this tension that will never be resolved. Our task is to integrate our bodily awareness with our cognitive insights. Only then can we escape magical thinking, explanatory structures that do not help to find meaning or being seduced by bodily signals that we overinterpret.

Getting to know your grief

In any loss, we try to understand what we have lost or what this loss means to our lives. Therefore, the IPM works with the point that we must get to know our grief and become aware of how it affects body and mind. From here, we can find a meaningful way to grieve and express the grief. Furthermore, the point of the IPM is that grief is a lifelong process of revisiting thoughts, memories, and perhaps even feelings of anger, shame, guilt, or resentment, and while these revisits are likely to diminish over time, they do not necessarily ever go away completely.

The IPM also points out that rather than putting grief behind us, unfinished or unlived aspects of our lives that we constantly think about or return to can tell us something about our existential values and our lives. It is only by bringing them to light that we can unfold them and live by them. The IPM points out that we must all take responsibility for our own feelings about loss and grief, because otherwise, we impose them on others. As we come to know our grief, they offer an opportunity to examine how our loss continues to define our lives and how the anger, shame, guilt, or other emotions limit our freedom or keep us isolated from others. Loss invites us to reflect on our assumptions about the world and our values in life and how we can live closer to the life we want without the past imposing too many limitations. Our ability to put into perspective the immediate physical and emotional sensations here and now gives us the freedom to respond to the world around us and shape our lives.

Text box 5.6   Existential reflection—the freedom to take responsibility for grief

- What do my losses tell me about my freedom as a human being?
- What do my losses tell me about the limits of my responsibility?
- What constructs of meaning do I have about loss that I cannot control? Do I call that fate? God's will? Do I blame myself or others? Something else?
- How are these reflections helpful in understanding my own existence and being in the world?

The unfinished and the unlived

It's a myth
that we can work with our losses in a way
so we can put them behind us forever.

We will always return to old losses and grieve them again as we mature and cognitively understand a little more of what the loss means to us and our lives. This also means that we may carry feelings of anger, regret, guilt, or blame with us from our loss. These unfinished thoughts and feelings can continue to tease us existentially if we do not find a good balance in how they affect us as we try to reconnect with ourselves and with life. This is why we keep going back to aspects of our loss and grief that have not landed in a good place—not because we did not put the grief behind us, but because existentially, we are trying to find a better balance in the tensions that have been opened up.

It is not uncommon to meet grieving individuals who feel that the loss has left them wishing for conversations that never happened, things they wish they had said or asked or talked about before the loss. After the loss or breakup, it is now up to the grieving person to end these open thoughts and feelings or the unlived conversations and connections within themselves.

Integrating feelings of anger, guilt, shame, or blame serves more than one purpose. It seems that it takes a lot of energy and can lock our minds into certain thought patterns or hinder a dynamic process in our grief. We all know it. Our thoughts keep circling around some issues without being able to completely find an end to the thoughts and feelings. When we can find a way to understand and integrate the thoughts and feelings better, it helps us to make our thoughts flow more freely and give the processing of grief a dynamic boost. The problem is that often, these thoughts and feelings revolve around something that can be difficult to talk to others about, as they are closely linked with anger, guilt, shame, self-criticism, or other intense feelings that we may consider unacceptable. The IPM brings awareness to these past losses that can follow us through life, not as something we just have to get rid of. When we give attention and conscious reflection to these losses and that they also play a role in a grieving process, it can help us navigate and keep the balance in grief while we better integrate the losses and the grief.

Text box 5.7   Existential reflection—cognitive flexibility

- Are there certain situations or incidents in which you have had to carry intense emotions such as anger, guilt, blame, or shame? What situations have triggered these feelings in you?
- When you revisit these situations and feelings, is it possible for you to gain a sense of acceptance and compassion in relation to the situation and yourself? Are there good reasons for feeling the way you do? That the situation turned out the way it did? Were there good reasons you decided or acted as you did?
- Is it possible to find a sense of cognitive flexibility and freedom of choice? What have you learned from the situation? What other reactions could you have chosen in the situation?
- If you had to give good advice to a friend in the same situation, what advice would you give?

The transformative potential of cognitive flexibility

The moment when our consciousness can stop
to fight reality,
we can begin to learn about our grief

and regain our inner flexibility.
From this place in the mind,
we can overcome the consequences of our loss.

Based on all the different cognitive expressions of grief that are described in this chapter, the IPM places it as a central task in the cognitive dimension to understand what we have lost and to get to know our grief. We distort our thinking in grief and create magical thoughts, we attach meaning to the loss and construct our own reality, and we use our body's sensory memory in our memories and daydreams about the lost, but sometimes, we also overinterpret the body's signals and think they are intuitions or truths. This chapter has described how grief plays out in our minds and in our attention. The IPM points out that we can use our awareness to observe our own mind and become aware of how our thought processes and our bodies affect the grieving process and sometimes help or hinder the integration of our grief. Old thought patterns and assumptions can hinder our grieving process, and there is a risk that we get stuck when we lack flexibility. A main point of the IPM is that we can build up an inner freedom if we become aware of our grief, and this makes us less vulnerable. When we understand that through our attention and metacognition, we can become aware of the grief process itself and that it plays an important role that we get to know our own grief, we can take responsibility for it. When we know the fluctuations of our grief and different thought patterns and feelings, our attention can open a new space, and such a space allows us to help make choices about our grief process.

When we reflect on the way we grieve, we can discover aspects we may not be so aware of, i.e., the thought patterns that shape our thinking and the values we orientate ourselves toward. From an existential perspective, this means that we open ourselves to more freedom in the mind so that we can take responsibility for our grief and become open to where the grief takes us. Thus, we can develop a better understanding of who we are or who we would like to develop into. It might even teach us about how to meet other grievers. Because grief is a learning process for the brain (and an existential learning process), we can approach others with an open attitude and interest in what they are going through instead of thinking we have an idea how it is to walk in their shoes.

This openness can also be called cognitive flexibility, which means the ability to flexibly switch between different perspectives in our thinking or the mental ability to adjust the content or even the activity of thinking itself when necessary. The awareness of thinking (phenomenology) and our thinking about thinking (metacognition) can help us with the flexibility to avoid overthinking or change the content so that we spend less energy on counterfactual thinking, i.e., on fighting reality. It can help us regulate our thinking and emotions in grief, increase our tolerance for negative emotions, and even improve our communication skills while grieving.

The importance of cognitive flexibility can be understood as the difference between an old oak tree with very strong branches and deep roots compared to a palm tree with very few branches and thin, spaghetti-like roots. During a violent storm, one would think that the old oak with its strong branches provides the best shelter. However, the strong oak is also stiff, and during strong winds, this stiffness is challenged, and the branches can break. The palm tree, on the other hand, with its thin branches, is more flexible and able to move in pace with the storm and thus remain intact. When we grieve, even the smallest adjustments and changes will help us form and reinforce new thought pathways in the brain so that we gradually evolve in step with the process.

Central points in Chapter 5

- Every grieving process is unique because it is inextricably linked to our bodily senses, our emotional state, and our mental processes.
- The cognitive dimension in the IPM is about our cognitive processes and bodily memory.
- When we grieve, we attach meaning to the loss, which is part of a larger process of trying to create meaning in our lives.
- We are used to thinking that grief shuts down our brain, but in reality, loss and grief pave the way for major changes in our neural activity and create new paths of thought, which, along the way, transform our outlook on life and being in the world.
- In research on the brain in grief, grief appears to be a learning process.
- During the grieving process, we think a lot about what we have lost, we immerse ourselves in memories, and our consciousness is even active in thinking about our grieving process and how we will grieve.
- Our bodies are carriers of our life history, experiences, emotions, memories, indeed, our entire brain, and it is with our bodies that we meet the world and communicate and interact with others. Therefore, the body is also a large part of the consciousness that mourns.
- We struggle with the impossible question of the meaning of our loss. Our consciousness works with two different languages: the explanations we all share as humans dealing with causation of the loss and the understanding of the loss that is formed through meaning making, using the unique meaning structures we each carry to create meaning in the world.
- It is a myth that we can work through our losses in a way that puts them behind us forever. And it is also a myth that this should be the purpose of our grief. We carry our losses with us and revisit them in our minds again and again to constantly integrate them better into life and understand their meaning from new perspectives in life.

- In the IPM, it is described how freedom and responsibility in the cognitive dimension are found in the tension between looking for both reflexive awareness and bodily awareness. The more we get to know our grief, the more freedom we will experience in grief and the easier we can make choices and take responsibility for our grief process.
- Achieving cognitive flexibility in our grief can be a great help in navigating the cognitive dimension of grief.

Interlude: Ann's struggle with the cognitive dimension of loss

Ann began to realize that her own emotional lack of freedom, her awareness and thinking about missing a "home" or a place in life was perhaps the biggest challenge to her personal freedom. She became interested in reading autobiographies of strong women with whom she could identify, and she felt inspired. She could see now that she had always been very focused on her work and all the things that she could afford due to her busy work life. When she was in a bad mood, she even thought that her financial stability, the recognition of colleagues, status, and extravagant lifestyle were all about having an identity. Now, however, she felt more and more vulnerable and at the mercy of a body that no longer seemed to just want to live that way or that she needed to find more meaningful attachments. She was again in touch with the losses in her childhood, thinking about her mother and regrieving the losses and how difficult it had all been. It was as if she was reconstructing the understanding of her life, but now with the sensitivity to see more layers of vulnerability and rootlessness than she had seen before. It opened up a completely new understanding of herself and her life but also of a loneliness that, up until now, she had avoided feeling.

In the Center for Grief and Existential Values, we asked Ann to reflect on the fixed assumptions and thought patterns that she had arranged her life around. She had avoided thinking about her vulnerabilities by being very focused on her working life and the materialistic things she had afforded for herself. She became aware that a large part of her identity was based on this feeling of having achieved what she wanted in life: financial stability, recognition, status, and having an interesting and exciting job. The focus in her reflections was increasingly on understanding why this loss of a relationship affected her so deeply, getting to know her body in a new way during menopause, and acknowledging and taking responsibility for the sensitivity and vulnerability she experienced. It was new for her to get in touch with her childhood losses and to have to regrieve them again. There were completely new talks about whether she could learn anything from her losses and how they also could help inform her search for feeling at home.

Chapter 6

The social dimension. How can I be connected?

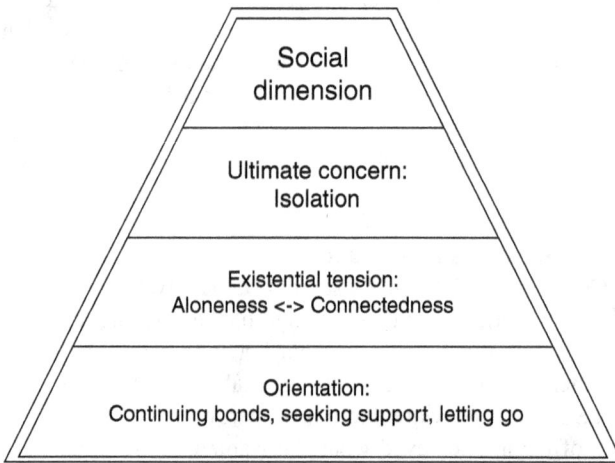

Figure 6.1 The social dimension of the IPM depicted as the segment of a pentagon containing the ultimate concern of isolation, the existential tension between aloneness, and connectedness and some directions.

In the ancient Greek myth of Orpheus and Eurydice, Orpheus captivated everyone with playing the lyre and his songs about his grief. No one could resist his beautiful melodies. Orpheus was the son of Apollo, and he could move both humans and gods with his song. The myth says that Orpheus fell in love with Eurydice, a woman known for her beauty and grace. Orpheus married Eurydice and was very fond of her. But Eurydice was bitten by a snake while she was dancing, and she died instantly. Confused from his grief, Orpheus decided to descend to Hades, the god of the underworld, to retrieve his wife. While no living person had succeeded in entering the underworld, Orpheus played so heartbreakingly and seductively that even Hades was moved and

DOI: 10.4324/9781003499060-6

let him pass to take back Eurydice. However, Orpheus had to obey one condition: he could not turn to look at her as they left the underworld. Only a few steps from the light, where Eurydice would turn into a living woman again, Orpheus lost confidence that things would go well and he turned to see if Eurydice was with him. He thus sent her right back to the captivity of Hades forever. Eurydice died a second time, and this time, at the sight of her husband.

(Source: Wikipedia)

This story from Greek mythology about Orpheus and Eurydice is among the most frequently told, and it is featured in numerous works of literature, operas, ballets, films, paintings, and poems. Still relevant today, the myth of Orpheus and Eurydice speaks to us of the existential tension between holding on and letting go. For many grieving individuals, this very tension can be difficult to balance while feeling stretched between a beloved past and an unknown future. We can experience it by refusing to acknowledge the reality of loss, holding on to a deceased person's belongings, or even holding on to dreams or visions that have defined us though they are no longer attainable. We can also be confronted with it when we experience loneliness because our lives were so defined by the relationship that is now lost. Or when we look for a way to honor our dead while at the same time struggling to live our lives for the living. Finding a balance between letting go of something valuable and holding on to the essence of what was lost has proven to be a very complex task. This tension can be difficult to navigate, and consequently, there is a temptation to either hold on and thereby deny the loss or to let go completely and try to avoid the loneliness or pain of the loss.

This chapter describes the social dimension of the IPM. It is about how grief plays out in social relationships but also about the relationship or connectedness to the person or thing we lost. For some, the experience of existential loneliness becomes a great challenge in grief. At the same time, the dimension describes social structures in grief such as traditions and rituals. Existentially, the dimension is linked with the question of "how can I be connected?"

When we express our grief, we show the world who we are

We express our grief. We do it when we talk about grief with others, but we also do it in all the traditions, rituals, and ceremonies we have developed in connection with death and loss. As a society, we have cultural and collective mourning practices. We mourn on the internet and pay tribute to famous people with gatherings, flowers, and funeral processions. We express our loss by erecting headstones, arranging funerals, organizing memorial services, or even holding on to a special memento or object that reminds us of what we have lost. We get a tattoo or wear a wedding ring in a necklace, which carries traces of what we have lost so that it can resonate in our body and we feel close to what we have lost. We embed the continued existence of the dead in our lives by displaying pictures and marking a special day annually. Even in everyday experiences like the sunrise, a certain type of fruit or flower connects us to the lost love, or a specific song serves as a reminder that keeps the memory alive.

> The lost, in its absence, becomes a constant presence.

In the affinity we have lost, connectedness can never quite be fulfilled again, yet it is as if we keep trying to make it whole or close a void in our minds. In our living connections, new threads of love are constantly being spun and lived out, whereas the love in our lost connections is defined by an emptiness that can become very complex with all its unlived possibilities. Grief shows us what is important to us, and now, we look for how we can live out or express these lost opportunities. It can even feel like never-ending work. We express grief because it feels like expressing love for what we have lost. We may even feel obligated to express this love and begin to look for ways to live out the lost opportunities.

> It can feel like
> it becomes an inner ethical demand for us to go through the grief,
> to express the love for what we have lost,
> to give back some of the love we received or feel within us.

It may even feel as if we are looking for ways to give the unlived a life and perhaps fulfill the potential of the lost, just as we name a fundraiser after a deceased or dedicate literature or art to a sick person. Sometimes, this expression of love becomes an idealization of the lost because it does not speak back to us, and we have to carry the love and the connectedness alone.

> We express ourselves through our grief
> and honor all that we have gained from what we lost.
> It can feel like a kind of life's work.
> However, it is also a way of looking for an expression of who we are.
> The expression of grief now becomes an expression of our authentic self.

If we do not honor the lost, we feel like we are failing at connectedness, and then we end up failing ourselves and feeling dead inside. That is why it is so important for us to express our grief and that the grief is acknowledged. However, there are naturally big differences between having to live without a spouse or a body part or living without a vision or a value that gave us a sense of connection to life and the future.

Grief as supreme expression of life?

The Danish philosopher Knud Ejler Løgstrup (1905–1981) wrote about our attachment to others by talking about *the ethical demand*. He explains that "We never have anything to do with another human being without holding some portion of his life in our hands" (Løgstrup, 1956/1997). This is what Løgstrup called an *ethical demand*—not only to do onto others what you would like them to do to you, as the golden rule in the Bible prescribes. Løgstrup would also say that we must always do our best toward others, even if they cannot show us the same respect.

Løgstrup points to our subjectivity, our essential humanness, where we are placed in a certain society or group and where we depend on the love of others in order to develop. In this light, he defined the concept of *sovereign life expressions*. A sovereign life expression is a basic utterance that is not subject to decision-making or even deliberation but is spontaneous and basic to humans, such as love, trust, or patience.

Although Løgstrup did not mention it, it is in the philosophical background of the IPM that grief can also be understood as a sovereign expression of life. Grief is a basic, essential, and spontaneous expression in life, which is important for our being in the world and understanding of life.

We do not express grief just because of the pain or suffering.
Like love, grief presents itself with an ethical demand
to be expressed, recognized, understood, and respected.
We do not express it just as an ultimate form of love
but also as a way of expressing ourselves.
In short: My grief tells you who I am, and therefore, it is very important
to me.

Perhaps this is also what the existentialist writer Albert Camus points to in his famous novel *The Stranger* (Camus, 1942/1989). In the story, we meet Meursault just as he learns that his mother is dead. We follow him during his grief but learn that he does not show the usual signs of grief and does not seem to mourn the loss of his mother—at least until, on a confusing and fatal day of intense heat and bright sunlight, Meursault murders a man on the beach. The novel ends with Meursault being sentenced to public beheading, and when a priest tries to save Meursault from the apathy he has displayed throughout the story, Meursault rejects the priest. *The Stranger* is considered one of the great works of existential thought, as Meursault experiences the indifference of the universe and feels completely abandoned by humanity. Camus shows us with Meursault's alienation that a life without sorrow is not desirable. A life without sorrow would mean a life of indifference and without love and connectedness. If we don't dare to feel the sadness, then we lose something of our humanity.

Precisely because grief is so closely connected to what is meaningful to us, to our love, to our identity, grief can be considered sovereign and untouchable.

The social dimension of grief

In 1895, the Norwegian painter Edvard Munch painted the painting *Death in the Sick Room*. It portrays the despair and anguish that Munch experienced as a child when his sister Sophie was dying of tuberculosis. Munch depicts how all the family members find themselves in the hospital room while his sister struggles with death. The remarkable thing about the painting is that all the family members are placed in the same room, but they stand far apart and look lonely in their despair.

> Although they share the same loss,
> they are isolated in their grief.

This is not an uncommon portrayal of grief in the social dimension. Grief unfolds as much between people as it does within the individual. Grief is located in our social relationships, and it is also part of the culture we live in, the society or community we are part of, and our social environment places expectations and rules for our grieving behavior. Grief is considered by many to be a deeply relational matter. This means that grief is understood in relation to who or what has been lost, the connection you had to what was lost, the role it played in our lives, and thus what kind of relationship we now have to live without. It also means that most of us suffer relationally when we experience loss. In the relational dimension, the initial loss will often be followed by secondary relational losses because we feel isolated, unable to communicate our pain, or we feel not understood by others. It feels like an additional loss when grief isolates us—inside and out. Suddenly, we find ourselves alone on a deserted island of grief. The island floats in the sea of loss, and we feel disconnected from society, from our culture, or even from our friends.

> We do not know if it is the grief that cuts us off and challenges us
> so that we cannot convey the pain to the others
> or whether it is society or culture that creates a distance from the grieving
>   person
> because grief is so painful to witness.
> It is most likely both.

The social dimension of grief deals with many different aspects of our relationships but also our tendency to social withdrawal, how we express grief and try to communicate it to others, and the cultural practices and mourning rituals we have. The American professor and grief researcher Kenneth Doka has pointed out that we tend to overlook the importance of others, the community, and social processes in the expression of grief. Our cultural and collective mourning practices and memorial rituals play a huge role in our grief and how we express it (Averill & Nunley, 1988; Bowlby, 1980; Doka, 2023; Kellehear, 2000; Walter, 2008). In our Western culture, for example, we accept that we express our grief in relatively close connection with our lost; however, if we continue to express our grief, we no longer tolerate this expression. Now, grief is understood as a personal problem we have. At the same time, if our surroundings and society do not recognize our loss or our way of expressing grief, then we are left alone with the grief and might even feel ashamed of it. We might even try to hide our grief. Now, we don't get the support or recognition from others that we so badly need. Hence, the social dimension of grief is very central.

To shed light on the social aspects of grief, there are studies that examine the social support and the unwritten *grieving rules* and mourning practices that are part of our communities. What is called *grieving rules* or *grieving participation* is especially about how we talk about our feelings when we are in grief and how we show compassion and give each other space to express grief and how we let others participate in our grief (Hansen et al., 2023). It is unwritten and implicit social rules that help dictate with whom the griever can talk about the grief and share the strong feelings and whether the grief can be expressed publicly. The environment also uses the implicit rules of grieving to sanction the bereaved person's behavior and ask about the loss or refrain from asking about it. If the grief is not recognized or the grieving rules become too narrow, the griever is deprived of the opportunity to grieve, Doka explains in his texts (Doka, 2023). This means that the griever does not get space to express their grief or receive social support and thus the relief and connectedness that come from having the opportunity to express their grief.

These implicit rules of grieving play a role in what we consider to be socially accepted and tolerated around the expression of grief. The implicit rules of grieving even play a role in how we as a society plan support for bereaved persons. Many support groups work from ideas that are in accordance with the rules of grieving and that sharing grief is healing. However, just as many healing rituals we find in the social dimension, just as many challenges we find in expressing our grief when the rules of grieving become too narrow. It is therefore of great importance to the griever which grieving culture and which grieving rituals are socially sanctioned by the surroundings. Grieving rules affect which memorial and grieving rituals are acceptable and the emotional and cognitive processes of the loss. Further, it is also important whether the griever feels connected to others in the social circle and how quickly social life can be reestablished.

The social dimension of grief is related to the question of how to let go or hold on to what is lost, but it is also about the ultimate existential concern of isolation or aloneness. As humans, we live in an existential tension between the need to belong to a group or a community where we feel recognized and valued. On the other hand, we also need to be alone and make the choices that are important to our own lives, even if it sometimes means we have to step out of our group. Therefore, the social dimension in the IPM is linked to the ultimate concern of isolation and the fear of being alone and the existential tension in experiencing the connectedness that we would like to have.

> After a significant loss, we are confronted with
> the existential void of loneliness and isolation.
> Here, it is easy to feel disconnected and alone
> when we are pushed into our own company and existential being.

We feel that our love and connectedness in life are threatened, that our roles in life are destroyed, or that our values are invalidated. There is no solid ground to stand on. It can be a very lonely place to be, and most of us dread the painful sense of emptiness and existential isolation we encounter there.

Text box 6.1   Existential reflection—between isolation and connectedness

- How do you express who you are through your grief?
- What grieving rules do you experience in your community? Do others have expectations about how you express your grief?
- How do you honor the connectedness to what or whom you have lost?
- Do you understand your sadness as an expression of yourself?
- Do you isolate yourself in your grief, or is it the others who distance themselves from you?
- What difficulties do you experience in feeling connected to others in your grief?

Solitude

Moses, Jesus, Mohammed, Buddha—they all did it. Just as Jesus did after the Last Supper with his disciples, he sought solitude to find himself and prepare for what was to come. Buddha was alone under his tree when he found enlightenment and a deeper understanding of life. These examples were later shared with others, thus creating millions of followers. With solitude as a common recipe, they have reported positive results such as improved sanctity and spirituality and the feeling of oneness with God, nature, or the universe. It has also been described that famous writers such as Henry David Thoreau, Emily Dickinson, Rudyard Kipling, and Franz Kafka did so. They sought solitude in order to find space for their creative processes and embody it in artistic writings, which would later be read by millions and praised for their human insight. The philosopher Nietzsche was known to walk alone for hours to develop his philosophical ideas, which later influenced many texts, and the walk can still be found today under the name "Nietzsche sentier." And even Kierkegaard liked solitude and pointed out that the search for solitude is a sign of depth in a person (Kierkegaard, 1849/1941). So as painful, lonely, and potentially harmful as solitude may seem, it has also been called a vital phenomenon that seems to be fruitful in religious, spiritual, creative, artistic, and personal processes.

It is a great paradox
that despite our human needs for companionship, connection, and belonging,
it seems we can benefit from solitude, too,
to find inner peace and insight.

In loss and grief, one of the aspects we are most aware of is the experience of abandonment and of feeling alone. In the grief literature, this is almost exclusively referred to as a negative aspect of loss, and here, it is pointed out that it is a struggle to find a new way of living without the lost. It can pertain to a person who is no longer here or who changes due to illness or accident or that we have to find out how to live without a job or a vision that is taken from us.

In philosophy, several hundred years before Christ, Aristotle coined what is called the principle of individuation as a criterion that distinguishes one person from others of the same species (Durant, 1926). In Jungian analytical psychology, individuation is a process characterized by the individual self developing from an undifferentiated unconscious and immature psyche into an integrated, well-functioning whole, which can step out of its attachment to a group or family and transcend its self-absorption and preoccupation with something outside itself. This was later described by the psychoanalyst Donald Winnicott (1958) with the words that if we want to avoid ending up in inner loneliness and anxiety, we must absorb the support of the important people around us and build it into our personality. Only in this way can we develop the ability to tolerate loneliness. Winnicott argued that the person who has developed the ability to be alone will never truly be alone. But without this capacity, the person will always flee into social contact and cannot thrive in his own company (Winnicott, 1958). Lord Byron (1788–1824) also described solitude as the place where we are least alone (Byron, 1812–1818/2021), and in the poem *Paradise Lost*, the English poet John Milton (1608–1674) even notes that solitude is sometimes the best company (Milton, 1667/2003).

Thus, on the one hand, loneliness and isolation are described as some of our ultimate existential concerns, while on the other hand, it appears that solitude is necessary for us to develop our own personality and, in particular, to achieve personal maturity that can enable us to get more connectedness. In the social dimension of the IPM, the focus is precisely on this tension between loneliness and connectedness.

> Paradoxical as it may sound,
> several philosophers and theorists have put forward the idea
> that although solitude usually denotes loneliness,
> loneliness is also linked to the ability
> to be able to find connectedness.

Existential loneliness

> Few artists have captured the struggles and hardships of life in a more direct and raw way than the American poet and novelist Charles Bukowski (1920–1994). In his poem "No Place for That," he gives voice to the experience of a place in the human heart that is never filled. The poem can be read as expressing the existential experience that deep in the human heart, there is a longing for a connectedness that will never be fulfilled. It confronts us with an existential loneliness that we can try to escape but that will always remain a part of us (Bukowski, 1986/2002).

As humans, on the one hand, we strive to be unique. We long to be recognized and loved for the person we are and all that we are capable of. On the other hand, our striving to be unique will give rise to feelings of isolation and loneliness because we have to step out of the pack. The existentialist thinker Spinelli pointed out that here, our self-awareness reveals completely opposite needs that create a tension and become a major source of conflict within us (Spinelli, 2015). Our protection against loneliness is that we create connectedness to other people, and therefore, we often understand loneliness as a social problem.

> However, loneliness can also be understood as something
> that is related to our problems in expressing who we are and can
> create connectedness to ourselves, the times we live in,
> our culture, or even a common vision in society.

According to an existentialist mindset, we try to alleviate our basic and universal anxiety about isolation by forming relationships with others or a common cause or vision. We cling to others, the belief in a divinity, a value system, or a greater cause in order for this to bridge the gap between isolation and connectedness so that we can avoid the challenge of experiencing our own existential aloneness.

> Attachment gives us a sense of security,
> and connectedness gives us a sense of having an anchor in life
> or a meaning or purpose in life,
> which makes most of us feel better.

Attachments pull us away from isolation and ease our existential angst. For some people, this becomes a big challenge when a close person dies or we lose a sense of belonging. We are reminded of the feeling of loneliness when the bond with a loved one or a job held changes or children move away from home, contact with a family member becomes different, and many other losses we face. It can almost feel like we lose a part of ourselves and our identity because the other person, the role, the job, the vision stood between oneself and the feeling of existential loneliness. When we lose something that is meaningful to our sense of identity, we lose the resonance that has been in these meaning structures, and it will be experienced as if we also lose part of our connection to the world. We struggle with feeling isolated, and it feels like a threat to the self. When we face a loss, the world loses its familiarity, we are robbed of the values by which we navigate our existence, and we feel alienated and alone.

> In his poem "Desert Places," the American poet Robert Frost (1874–1963) beautifully expresses how the fear of void and isolation is not something only connected to the infinitely deserted and cold spaces between the stars. This same anxiety can also be felt in ourselves when we sense our aloneness (Frost, 1933/1969).

Isolation, loneliness, or broken connections are very difficult and anxiety-provoking parts of human existence. It is both about the feeling of loneliness and isolation from others but also about an inner feeling of separation from oneself. While our social relationships help us as a buffer against the fear of being alone, it is not certain that we have secured a good understanding of our individuation or developed our personality or authenticity. Yalom says that "Our self-consciousness sentences us to meet our existence naked and alone" (Yalom, 1980). He described the need to gain insight into unknown sides or fears within himself to feel more whole or more connected to himself.

The lack of connection to our own self
and our lack of authenticity
is a frequent topic in modern psychotherapy.

Living the question: How can I be connected?

The French philosopher Paul Ricoeur (1913–2005) developed a theory of the human self in which he showed how the development of our sense of self is inherently dialogic (Ricoeur, 1992). From the moment we are born, it is other people who take care of us, who keep us alive, who introduce us to a community with language, customs, and traditions. In this way, we become part of the human family. Thanks to everything we learn from others and owe to others, we can develop a sense of who we are. And the paradox is that even in our most intimate, innermost "selves," we find the presence of the others. Thus, Ricoeur explains, we develop as a sense of "myself as another." But this is also the basis for developing empathy and a sensitivity toward other people's suffering (Ricoeur, 1992).

When we have suffered a loss, we each look for a way to live with our loss and to give the grief an authentic expression.

In the existential processes of loss
most people experience feeling alone
and even deeply isolated in their own existence.

In this feeling of isolation, we reach out to others and want to be taken out of the suffering, and although that might ease some of the pain, there is no one who can carry the burdens of our lives for us. No one can undergo the grief process for us, and no one can die for us. The existential process of grief requires that we ourselves look for ways to take responsibility for our reaction to the loss and look for our own expression of grief. Here, we feel the burden of our own life and the weight of creating our own meaning. It can be painful, but this confrontation also has the potential to strengthen us and enable us to make individual choices and thereby further develop our own selves.

Integration of past and future

A client had sought contact after she had lost her business. She mourned her business and her financial status but also having to let go of a vision and dream in life. There was so much unfulfilled potential that she did not know how to live with the losses. In the conversation, we tried a little exercise: imagine that you are standing on a timeline in a field of tension, where one end is your past life with your company and the other end, which also pulls at you, is your future with a new working life. Every day, both ends of this tension pull at you. You want to take some of your old life with you into your new future, but you cannot take all of it with you. You have to make decisions every day about how to continue and how to let go of some of your old vision. This is a process that takes time, and some decisions take longer than others. What the process requires of you is that you make the necessary decisions one by one. The exercise gave her a clearer picture of the process she was going through, and the conversation made her feel like she was gradually finding a balance in a complex task.

> In the IPM, a central task in grief is to express the grief
> and honor what was lost
> and, thus, integrate past and future.

It is said that grief is a time when we get ready for the rest of our lives. We get attached to what we care about and learn to hold on to it, and in time, we also have to learn to let it go again. British psychologist John Bowlby wrote in the last century about making and breaking these emotional bonds (Bowlby, 1980). Here, he put forward the theory of attachment and our innate ability to form an emotional bond with others. Bowlby also studied the reactions when an emotional bond was severed, and he described how the nature and quality of the emotional bond determine the response to the loss. In attachment theory, Bowlby explained that we form attachments because of our biological instinct to seek security. Our social bonds become a framework we keep our everyday life in and also get the support we need. Over time, these attachments not only make up our love lives, but they also shape our lives and our personalities. Bowlby studied the attachment style developed in the individual during childhood, and here, it became clear that some people form more secure attachment to others, while others form insecure attachment patterns based on the internal representations to build relationships. Most of us have formed a predominantly secure attachment pattern in which we have learned to rely on others to provide reassurance, support, and comfort. This has also enabled us to develop a positive self-image, because others acknowledge us and show us that we have value. Yet a significant number have primarily formed a more insecure attachment style, resulting in difficulty trusting others to provide reassurance and support, and this therefore creates a more negative worldview. If a person has learned that others are not necessarily trustworthy, the chances are higher that he or she will be much more stressed when faced with challenges, as there is not necessarily hope that others will help. Bowlby saw in his research that when we face separation from attachment figures, we respond to this separation with a sense of threat to our existence. As a result, Bowlby believed that when we face the loss of something that connects us to life, we reorganize our internal working models of relationships to include loss and the realization that emotional bonds can be broken (Bowlby, 1980).

Mario Mikulincer and Philip Shaver, two American psychologists and researchers, have many years later followed up on Bowlby's early work with attachment theory and investigated the effect of attachment on our grief reaction (Mikulincer & Shaver, 2022). They also assess that the attachment we have to the lost is absolutely central to the reactions we have in grief. At the same time, attachment has an impact on our grieving process and what meaning we attach to the loss (Chapter 5) and how we regulate our emotions (Chapter 4). Accordingly, the IPM has a background in emotional bond research.

In the IPM, it is central
that our grief reaction is closely linked to how we were connected to what
   is lost
and how we can create connectedness in our grief process.

Although not described by Mikulincer and Shaver, we must assume that attachment theory is also at play when we face losses other than death. After all, we are also attached to an arm or a leg that we can lose. Or to the idea of becoming parents, even though we may have to face that this dream will not come true. The client who lost her business earlier in this chapter has been attached to her business and felt joy in it, which has helped to define her identity. The way we form our attachments will dictate how we connect with ourselves and others. Based on the attachment style we have learned, we form an emotional bond or form the basis of an existential attachment to ourselves, another person, to our job, a pet, our dreams, visions, etc. Therefore, it also suggests that our attachment style and existential attachment to what we have lost play central roles in our response to losing it. This attachment and existential connectedness plays a crucial role in finding a balance in holding on and letting go.

Text box 6.2   Existential reflection—how am I connected to what I have lost?

- How do you try to integrate past and future in your grief?
- How has the loss affected your understanding of yourself?
- How is your attachment to the lost expressed in your grief?
- How can you express your attachment to the lost in a meaningful way?
- How does your grief show who you are?

Continuation of the emotional bond

After the devastating floods in Baton Rouge, Louisiana, USA, in 2016, journalists reported that lost boxes of family photographs were among the most mourned items (Newby & Toulson, 2019). A woman standing outside her flooded home spoke of her grief over a tape recording of her late father's voice that had been washed away, noting, "I've never felt such a loss before." Our grief is given form through symbolic objects that belonged to a deceased or in the form of tombstones and small artifacts used to commemorate what we have lost. We are constantly finding new ways to commemorate and decorate grave sites. These are all attempts to hold on to the past, to recreate it and maintain continuity between the inner emotional bond and give it expression in the social, personal, and cultural world (Newby & Toulson, 2019).

> Mourning objects and memorial symbols show that we are willing to communicate about loss and death.
> We do not try to hide it or necessarily avoid it as a taboo,
> but we try to express our grief to others through rituals and symbols.

It seems that the symbols help us show our grief and acknowledge our loss, and through memorial symbols, we try to remain connected to the lost and create meaning in the loss itself. All these material, symbolic, ritualized expressions of loss capture the idea of the continuation of the emotional bond and show how much part of our culture it is to maintain a symbolic attachment to what we have lost.

In 1996, the American psychologists Klass, Silverman, and Nickman presented the theory of continuing bonds—the continuation of the emotional ties to the lost. Klass and his colleagues asked the grieving people they met about how they went about saying goodbye to their deceased. To this, the mourners replied that they maintained the connection to the deceased by holding on to meaningful things that reminded them of the lost person; by hanging pictures or lighting a candle, or by wearing or displaying symbolic objects such as jewelry or a scarf. Others had spent a long time finding the right headstone and planning a memorial service in the spirit of the deceased or other rituals to give their grief a framework and content (Klass et al., 1996). The theory turned upside down the earlier Freudian hypothesis that grief work involves letting go of the connection to the deceased and saying goodbye. In their interviews with bereaved people, it became clear to Klass and his colleagues that mourners, to a greater extent, work to maintain the connection instead of letting go of the bond with the deceased.

The continuation of the bond with the lost seems to support the grieving process, integrate the loss, and help the grieving person into the future. It could be said that the continuation of the emotional bond revolutionized the understanding of one of the most basic and central tasks in grief, namely our understanding of how we let go and hold on. This is represented in the IPM by an emphasis on finding a balance between finding ways to honor the lost and continuing the connectedness to it. At the same time, we must also look for ways to take responsibility for the transition to another future and even create connectedness to something new.

Grief is a tension between letting go and holding on

> The existential tension between holding on and letting go
> is a fundamental challenge in all love relationships.
> It is no different when we think about how to live with a loss.

"I owe it to him to grieve," said a mother after losing her son. She was tormented by the thought that no one would remember him in the long run, that his life would have not mattered, or that it would seem like she no longer loved him if she did not continue her grieving activities. Letting go of our love can be so deeply painful that we can have the feeling that we are losing the whole basis of our existence.

> The more quality in the love to the lost,
> the more this connectedness meant to us,
> and the deeper the grief will be
> because the grief reflects the lost value.

Therefore, the nature of grief is not different from love. It requires a balance between being connected to oneself and to the other in order for love to develop into a vital connectedness.

Form a picture in your mind of the image of a person holding on to their love like a drowning man would hold on to a piece of driftwood. This type of love connection is not likely to last. In a romantic relationship, the attraction and love for the other can fill us in such a way that we completely forget our own selves and our own needs and try to merge with the other person. In the long run, this will strain love because the partners dissolve themselves into each other, resulting in the destruction of love because now, there is no longer another person to love.

Another example is the love parents have for their children. The love can be so overwhelming that parents become engrossed in building their lives completely around the child and thus almost blur themselves out, and now, there is no longer a clear role model for the child to learn from and develop their personality in relation to.

Just as a sustainable love cannot look like a drowning man,
clinging to a piece of driftwood,
a sustainable grief cannot work
without the surviving finding their own way of living.

We cannot create an expression of grief if we have become one with the grief. There will be no space in us for the love and the grief to create resonance and from which we can honor the connectedness. Only when we experience a connectedness with ourselves can we look at our own grief and feel and honor love. From this space within ourselves, we can grieve. Instead, picture the image of "holding on": The open invitation from a hand reaching out to offer friendship. We are free to say "no thanks," but we can also accept the invitation because we choose to.

To honor what is lost and to commemorate what is no longer present, there must be an authentic, individual self. The more strongly we are connected to ourselves, the better we can tolerate the loss. This does not mean that it hurts less or that we should not practice letting go, but it means that we are still deeply rooted in ourselves, and the pain does not destroy the existential connectedness. It is precisely for this reason that the connectedness in love is characterized by a polarity that is about both letting go and holding on. This tension is a balance, as shown by the example of the open hand offering friendship. Just as it is the case when we raise children to be independent and free persons: our love must both provide shelter, support, and protection on the one hand and freedom to experiment and make mistakes on the other.

In grief,
connectedness must give space to let go of the lost
while also holding on to the love for it.

Text box 6.3   Existential reflection—connectedness

- How do you create the balance between being connected to yourself and to others?
- How do you find a balance in your grief between holding on to what you have lost and letting it go?
- Have you found a good way to honor your loss and mark the connectedness to what you have lost?
- Have you found good ways to connect with yourself after experiencing loss?

Longing—what does it want from me?

Longing has been shown in studies to be one of the most common emotions in grief. Longing for what was lost or for the way life used to be or longing for the reciprocated love that was evident before the loss or even longing for the me I used to be before the loss. Longing seems to be a way to connect to or capture something of what is no longer there. In this sense, longing marks the connection between the lost and the grieving person. The longing reflects the love for the lost person or object or even ourselves as we used to be. It seems obvious that the more love there is for the lost, the bigger a part of our daily life it was, the more longing there will be. Many grieving people describe this longing as painful and filled with sorrow and suffering. Still, others describe the thought of the lost as a comfort that eases the pain of loss.

> The joy of remembering is equal to the pain of longing.

In the IPM, it is a fundamental understanding that the tension between letting go and holding on is expressed in our longing. Longing is closely related to the connectedness to the past, but it can be argued that longing also points in the direction of the future. However, what might not be so obvious is that the concrete aspects of longing also give the person information about what can alleviate the suffering and reveal the person's wishes for the future. For example, the longing for love and intimacy after the loss of a spouse to illness, death, or divorce: this longing corresponds to what is wanted in the future. If the spouse cannot come back for obvious reasons, then it could be love in another form or for another person, a cause, a community, a belief, or something else.

> Longing is not only a sign of something missing;
> it can also be understood as a beacon of light and hope for the future
> because now I know what my inner self is calling for.

It is a difficult task to honor the past, to practice commemorative rituals, but also to live in the present and follow one's own path into a meaningful future. That is exactly what the balance in the tension between letting go and holding on is all about. If it is possible to allow ourselves to feel the pain of longing, we can discover that longing is the very connection between the past and the future. When we can listen to our longing, it can help steer us toward our future goals and lead us into the future.

Our longing contains information about what we want in the future,
the connectedness that we want to regain,
and this can be transformed into a direction for where we are going.

The person who lost their spouse and longs for love and intimacy may choose to look for a new connectedness or passion in life. Obviously, an answer to this longing can be falling in love with another person, but so can many other forms of love and passion in life: the love for a family and developing a deeper connection to them, seeing more friends and developing these relationships, the love of a cause to which one can be passionately devoted, or even falling in love with a new philosophy of life, a craft, art, literature, religion, nature, or many other passions that can answer our longing for connectedness. For many of us, seeking a deeper connectedness to ourselves will even answer some of the existential longing we experience or the existential loneliness we experience. A closer connection to ourselves helps us to reach closer to the authenticity that we also long so deeply for.

Text box 6.4   Existential reflection—longing

- What are you longing for?
- How can this longing be a guide to where you are going in the future? What do you want in life in the future?
- How can your longing help you into a deeper connectedness with yourself?
- How does your longing express your existential values?
- How can your longing help you get closer to your values in the future?

The transformative potential of connectedness

When we are in the womb, we are completely connected to and dependent on another person in order to grow. In childhood, we are completely dependent on parents or significant others in order to survive and reflect ourselves in in order to develop. When we first learn to separate ourselves from others, we start a process of independence, individuation, becoming ourselves.

This means that separation and isolation are both
something that we fear the most,
but separation is at the same time the very process
whereby we can become ourselves.

This is what this chapter has unfolded. Existentially, our personal development process can be seen as a process of separation or even one long process of loss. We are pressed into a tension between togetherness and isolation. This process becomes very apparent when we experience grief. If we are open to it, grief can become an existential demand to express our love for the lost but at the same time also a demand to express who we are and to be authentic about the pain that is in us. It is at the same time a process where we feel connected to something that can no longer be fully obtained while we seek connectedness with others, and we practice sharing feelings and vulnerabilities. It is very human to suffer from the fear that when we show our true feelings and vulnerabilities to others, it comes with a sense that this may also destroy us.

It makes us very vulnerable to show our true selves,
and the easy way out is
to seek isolation or create distance from others in our grief.
But if we look closely, loss opens up a space for connectedness.
It is when we dare to share our vulnerabilities that we open the space
for more connectedness and more authenticity in our relationships.

During this process, we will also remember the past and create a connection to the lost, but now, we have to carry it inside ourselves and not outside in a relationship. In this process, grief becomes timeless within us, and the connectedness creates a love that overcomes death—a resurrection in the mind of the griever, if you will.

Text box 6.5   Existential reflection—loss and separation

One of the differences between loss and separation is that loss is passive, but separation can also be active.

- Try to look back on your life and ask yourself who and what you have separated yourself from along the way.
- What did it mean to you?
- Can separation be both positive and negative for you?
- How have you been able to face the pain of separation?
- Have you gotten better at being separate from others over the years?

Central points in Chapter 6

- In grief, we show the world who we are: we honor our loss and express what is meaningful connectedness to us.
- In the social dimension of the IPM, grief unfolds as much inside the person as outside the person and between people, within the social ties we have, but also as part of a culture, a society, or a community that sets expectations and rules for mourning behavior.
- In grief, we navigate the tension between holding on to what we hold dear or find meaningful and letting go of what can no longer be lived.
- As humans, we live in an existential tension between the need for connectedness, i.e., to belong to a group or community where our existence is recognized and understood, and the importance of being able to be alone, express ourselves, and make our own choices. This tension comes into play in grief.
- Grief can make us feel isolated within ourselves but also in our surroundings. It can be hard to feel connected when we are grieving.
- Facing our existential aloneness is difficult but necessary to develop ourselves as free and authentic people.
- The attachment we had to what was lost influences the way we grieve our loss. Similarly, our connectedness to ourselves influences the way we are able to seek connectedness with other people.
- The continuing bonds theory explains why it is important to maintain a meaningful connection to the lost through rituals, objects, and traditions. The theory did away with the Freudian idea that grief work is about letting go and showed why holding on is just as important.
- The existential tension between holding on and letting go is a fundamental challenge in all love relationships. It is no different when we think about how to live with a loss.
- Our longing is the connection between what we have had and now miss and what we would like to have in the future. We can live that connection when we realize that longing contains information about our future that can be transformed into a direction for where we are going.
- Grief has a transformative potential, which, among other things, is about separation being necessary to develop. We have done it many times since we were in the womb, through our childhood, and all the way through adulthood.

Interlude: Ann's struggle with the social dimension of loss

In the months that followed, Ann found herself reading her old diaries and letters that she had exchanged with friends and family over the years. She even looked on social media for old friends and corresponded with some of them to find out where they were and how their lives had progressed. She was curious to mirror her own life in theirs, as it felt like she had left her whole childhood and youth behind to move forward. Now, it helped her reflect on her own history and the thoughts that she had felt unwanted and not at home in this world from the beginning of her life. She had put all her talents and energy into building a safe place for herself and building a stable and secure position. Now it became evident to her that her entire career was completely based on her own performance, and suddenly, it felt lonely. She had not wanted to be dependent on other people, and she had not wanted to feel vulnerable by putting her fate in someone else's hands. She began to realize that even in friendships and romantic relationships, she would never admit to vulnerability or dependence. She wondered if this was also why she had never wanted to have children herself. Underneath the feeling of having accomplished something, she also felt a deep longing to experience a deeper connectedness. It was a huge challenge for her to have to accept that she had probably made some choices in life based on being afraid of becoming dependent on someone or rejected by someone. Her independence used to make her feel strong, and now, instead, it began to bring her into contact with a sense of loneliness and sadness because there was no balance in it. She suddenly felt homeless again, as she had when her mother died. There even was a deep longing within her for a fulfilling relationship that could provide her with some security and shelter while she went through this menopause process. Yet she also felt that she was not at all ready for a relationship because her body was in a transitional phase, and besides, it would distract her from all the inner work she was doing.

In the Center for Grief and Existential Values, we talked with Ann about the connectedness she was looking for and encouraged her to not look for it in a narrow sense but increase her awareness about where to find it. It turned out that Ann also felt it in spending time with good friends, and it became clear to her how big a part of her life these friendships were and how they helped her feel connected to life. Gradually, she practiced deepening some of these connections.

Chapter 7

The spiritual dimension.
Can I believe in life again?

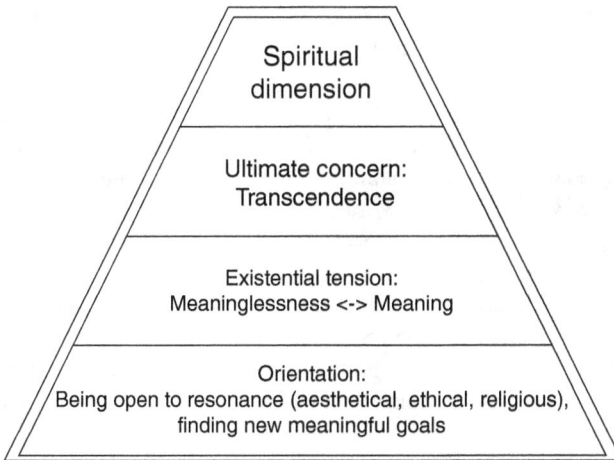

Figure 7.1 The spiritual dimension of the IPM depicted as the segment of a penta-gon containing the ultimate concern of transcendence, the existential tension between meaninglessness and meaning, and some directions.

The song "Vincent" by Don McLean (1972) is the story of one of the most famous paintings in the world: *The Starry Night*, painted by the Dutch painter Vincent van Gogh (1853–1890). In the lyrics, the singer describes how the painting speaks to him because it is painted in a way that makes him feel that the artist knows his suffering. He describes how the pain and suffering in van Gogh's paintings are transformed into a form of loving consolation. In the chorus of the song, McLean sings how he finally understands how van Gogh, with his paintings, tried to help people find freedom. But despite the great love that was in van Gogh's suffering, he was not recognized in his own time. The painter took his own life like a tragic love story. And McLean concludes with directly addressing the painter and telling him that he was a human being too beautiful to live in this world (McLean, 1972).

DOI: 10.4324/9781003499060-7

Vincent van Gogh's life was marked by disappointments, poverty, loss, and suffering. When he had difficulty finding his way in life, he only started painting at the age of 27. For the next ten years, until he took his own life at the age of 37, van Gogh painted his works in great poverty, suffered from syphilis, and had episodes of severe depression. His work was not recognized, and during his lifetime, he reportedly sold only one painting. *The Starry Night* was painted in the Saint-Paul-de-Mausole "lunatic asylum" in 1889, a year before his death, where van Gogh had voluntarily admitted himself. The view has been confirmed as being from his room in the psychiatric institution (Naifeh & Smith, 2011).

Great art has transformative potential. It is great art precisely because it speaks to us in a meaningful way that opens our senses to something new. The American composer Leonard Bernstein is quoted as saying, "A work of art does not answer questions, it provokes them; and its essential meaning is in the tension between the contradictory answers" (Bernstein, 1976). This is precisely what is pointed out in the IPM in relation to living the questions. This chapter is about the spiritual dimension in the IPM. When we have lost something valuable and we experience that life has lost its meaning, we often ask ourselves the question: "Can I believe in life again?"

Once touched by van Gogh's paintings, we not only recognize his very personal and authentic way of seeing the world, but we will also discover that he changes our way of seeing the world. Great art, philosophy, or literature opens us up to new ways of relating to the world. It transforms our potential to see, hear, sense, understand, and be in the world. This means that great art also transcends the time period of which it is a part. Johann Sebastian Bach (1685–1750) lived and worked 300 years ago, and although we cannot really imagine his daily hardships, many of us feel when we listen to his music that he knows and understands our innermost feelings. Bach lost 11 of the 20 children born in his two marriages, and his first wife died unexpectedly while he was away working. Are the deeply human and comforting tones in his music connected to the many losses he himself suffered? Or are they rooted in his deep Lutheran faith? Whatever explanation we may find, it is clear that the meaningfulness of Bach's music transcends time and space. And it is not just in van Gogh's paintings and Bach's music that grief and suffering are depicted, because many works of art and pieces of music are about loss and grief. A number of others are mentioned here in the book. When art reaches out to us and we are touched in a deeply personal way, art has the potential to become more deeply connected to aspects of ourselves that we may not have been in touch with or that we have not been able to convey or find resonance with in our social relationships. Art reaches us in a place where, as can be the case with grief, we lack words to express what we experience because we have not been in contact with it before or it seems bigger than our words can express. Art conveys access to a new space that this experience opens up in us, and from here, there is an opportunity to find new ways of being in the world.

Works of art are a personal and authentic way of responding to our existential, ultimate concern about meaning in life. But art is not the only way in which we encounter this existential dimension. Spiritual and religious traditions open to most people a space of transcendence in which we can find a personal answer to life's ultimate concerns: death, freedom, loneliness, and meaninglessness. Transcendence is a concept that comes from philosophy and theology, and it literally means "to climb beyond." It refers to aspects of life that cannot be measured objectively but only be recognized on the basis of our own experience. For example, we experience transcendence when we are in nature and we are suddenly overwhelmed by the feeling of nature's incredible beauty, the light playing in the treetops, or the way the sky's dramatic clouds are reflected in the sea, and right there, perhaps, feel the wonder of being alive. Moments of transcendence are often moments of awe and wonder, when words do not quite exist to express the greatness we experience.

> The spiritual dimension in the IPM is the dimension
> in which we answer our loss and grief by searching for
> meaning, faith, hope, trust, resonance, and transcendence.

The big question of spirituality

The search for a personal and authentic answer to transcendence or the ultimate existential concerns is, for some people, answered in the religious traditions. However, many people in the European countries struggle precisely with the spiritual and religious traditions. Despite the impressive advances in modern medicine since World War II, healthcare is probably one of the places where our suffering around loss, grief, and death is most embedded. Therefore, in the 1980s, an awareness grew in the healthcare system that not all the patient's needs are covered by a physical, psychological, or social approach alone but that a spiritual approach needed to be added. Since then, a growing body of literature has been published on the dimension of meaning and transcendence, particularly within the healthcare sector. In the English-speaking world, this dimension is often referred to as "the spiritual dimension" (Gijsberts et al., 2019; Balboni et al., 2017; Steinhauser et al., 2017). As confusion grew regarding the term "spiritual" and the question arose whether spirituality is the same as religion, it was proposed to work with a definition that could be agreed upon across the professional approaches. In a European context, a consensus definition of spiritual care was developed in 2011 in the European Association for Palliative Care:

> "Spirituality is the dynamic dimension of human life
> that relates to the way persons (individual and community)
> experience, express, and/or seek
> meaning, purpose, and transcendence,
> and the way they connect to the moment, to self, to others, to nature,
> to the significant, and/or the sacred."
>
> (Nolan et al., 2011)

In this definition, the spiritual-existential is seen as a universal human phenomenon that is dynamic in our lives. The term *spiritual* refers to the way we experience, express, and seek to engage with the ultimate concerns of death, freedom, loneliness, and meaninglessness. Loss and grief have the potential to activate the big existential questions about our mortality and the meaning of life. No human can live without meaning. Structures of meaning help us orient ourselves in life, and as existential thinkers such as Viktor Frankl and Irvin D. Yalom make clear, we need them to provide our personal and authentic responses to the existential concern of meaninglessness (Frankl, 1946/2006; Yalom, 1980). The same applies to the purpose, because as Nietzsche said in Viktor Frankl's formulation, "He who has a why to live can bear almost any how" (Frankl, 1946/2006). And Viktor Frankl discovered as a prisoner in Auschwitz during World War II that those of his fellow prisoners who had a purpose in life were significantly more likely to survive the hardships than those who had given up on life. For Frankl himself, the time in Auschwitz entailed a long struggle to be able to publish the book he had already written before the time in the concentration camp, *Man's Search for Meaning*. The manuscript for the book was destroyed when he was captured, but he managed to survive and write the book again. In the book, he describes that his deep sense of purpose and meaning helped him survive Auschwitz.

In addition to meaning and purpose, the definition of spiritual care mentions transcendence. "Transcendence" here refers to that which lies in our consciousness beyond our control and planning and perhaps beyond what we can put into words. The great works of art referred to in the beginning of this chapter all have this unique quality of transcendence: they speak to us from a place beyond our control. Although Bach was a very well-trained craftsman as a composer who knew exactly how to "compose" (i.e., put together) a piece of music according to the rules and tastes of his time, no one can explain why this music is still able to touch millions of hearts very deeply and even more intensely than that of other Baroque composers who lived 300 years ago and have long since been forgotten. But transcendence can also mean that someone is able to recognize that the individual I am as a human is not the center of the universe.

There is a beautiful saying ascribed to the Indian Nobel laureate, poet, writer, and painter Rabindranath Tagore (1861–1941) that expresses that the meaning of life is not putting ourselves and self-preservation at the center. Rather, the image is used of planting a tree whilst knowing that it will take so many years to grow and give shadow that the planter will never sit in its shade. Understanding the meaning of life is understanding transcendence.

Tagore (Goodreads)

It expresses how serving the love of humanity can be a transcendent goal in life, as it happens, in the healthcare system, and in many helping or caring professions. Transcendence is inextricably linked to the existential tension between meaning and meaninglessness, because it points to the fact that experiencing something as meaningful is not entirely something we can control or plan for ourselves. Many people who have suffered a loss may find solace in music. For example, some people find solace in Eric Clapton's song "Tears in Heaven," which he wrote after his four-year-old son died when he accidentally slipped out of a window in an apartment building in New York. Other people feel that their grief is mirrored in the raw and heartfelt words of Tom Waits in "Take It With Me," or perhaps it is the depth of Mozart's requiem that is able to carry them through their grief. However, no one can decide whether they will be deeply moved by one piece of music or the other. There is something mysterious about the way meaningfulness works in our lives, and we will return to that later in the chapter.

In the definition of what spirituality is, connectedness is also described. This shows how important a role connectedness plays in living a meaningful life. For some people, meaningful connection is found in a deep connectedness to other people or to nature. For others, the connection to something transcendent or sacred is the most meaningful connectedness in their lives. For a large part of the world's population, this connectedness is experienced as the sanctity in feeling connected to God. This is also called religiosity. Religiosity is a specific way of living out the spiritual dimension. However, it is not the only way. For some people, the spiritual dimension is rooted in a nonreligious philosophy of life, such as Buddhists and humanists, who do not believe in a higher power or a God but find meaning and purpose in life through a strong existential awareness and clear choices in relation to how life is lived. Many humanists have a strong commitment to freedom and to the goal of contributing to a more just and inclusive society in which no person or group is oppressed. Buddhism is a way of life that aims to live free from attachments but instead live with great compassion toward self and fellow creatures. Some people prefer to live out their search for meaning, purpose, and transcendence without attaching it to a particular frame of meaning. Although they would not call themselves religious and they might also have reservations about the word *spiritual*, their search for purpose and meaning is deeply authentic and human. And like all other people, they can be inspired by moments of transcendence.

At the same time, the central role of connectedness in the definition of spirituality makes us aware that there are many possible losses that can have a profound impact on the meaningfulness of our lives. Connectedness can be threatened or destroyed when a meaningful connection is lost. It can be the connection to a group, a congregation, a job, a common cause, and much more. It can even be the connectedness we experience to certain dreams we have in life. When the connectedness is lost or we have to give up the dream, it is followed by the experience of loss, and we react with grief. Therefore, our grief is about meaning, purpose, transcendence, and connectedness in the individual's life. Oscar Wilde wrote in a long letter from prison, which was later published as *De profundis* (Wilde, 1905/2015), "Where there is sorrow, there is holy ground."

> Grief can be called holy ground for the individual
> because it has an existential depth in it
> that is related to meaning, purpose, transcendence,
> and connectedness in the unique individual's life.

The spiritual dimension and its tensions

One day, Carlo asked one of the older men at the nursing home at which he was temporarily working on a research project whether he believed in life after death. The man had been a widower for many years. After a short pause, he said, "Of course there is no heaven and hell. All of this is nonsense that the church made us believe when I was young, and I said goodbye to these ideas a long time ago. Nevertheless, deep down, I am quite sure that I will meet my late wife again when I am no longer on this earth."

The spiritual dimension in IPM alludes to how, in our grief, we try to orient ourselves in the existential tension between meaninglessness and meaning. Meaning can be what we have learned early in life and accepted as a framework around how death and loss can be meaningful, but it can also be many aspects of life to which we create connectedness.

> When we experience loss, our understanding of the world can collapse,
> and the world suddenly looks like a cold, desolate, and meaningless place.

Meaninglessness is hard to endure. Our mind works in such a way that it tries to make sense of what has happened (as described in Chapter 5 on the cognitive dimension and construction of meaning). Our minds gravitate toward finding an explanation that can give us meaning because holding on to the meaninglessness of a loss is hard to tolerate. The old widower navigated between discarding his old framework of meaning and simultaneously having an intuitive and embodied hope that he might be reunited with his wife. Logically, it seems like a paradox to reject any idea of an afterlife and still believe in meeting a lost love.

On another occasion, Carlo asked his 23-year-old nephew if he thought his mother—who had died seven years earlier—was still around somewhere. His nephew replied, "I don't know. I hope I will see her again one day, but I don't know if I think it's even possible. That's why I don't think so much about it, because then, there is still the great consolation that there is a hope of seeing her again."

We navigate the existential tension between meaning and meaninglessness by combining thoughts and feelings on a continuum between knowing and believing. At one end of the continuum is scientific knowledge, with the certainty and solid foundation that this can provide. At the other end of the spectrum, there is the security and the solid ground that believing can bring forth.

Knowing here means seeking reliable knowledge and being skeptical of theories and stories that are too good to be true or are not based on solid scientific research. Scientific knowledge is not important for everyone. How people differ in this respect can be illustrated by the discussion of near-death experiences. For some people, the reporting of beautiful near-death experiences of thousands of people whose hearts temporarily stopped beating is enough to make them believe that the existence of heaven or an afterlife has now been proven. When this is integrated into their global framework of meaning, it can be of great comfort in making sense of the losses they have suffered. But others will react more skeptically and conclude that being close to death is the same as being almost pregnant: It does not exist. For some people, reliable knowledge is a lifelong search; others are easy to convince. People have different ways of dealing with life's ultimate concerns. A solid base of understanding means different things to different people.

For some, maintaining a particular worldview is seen as a matter of surrender. In the world's great religions (Judaism, Christianity, and Islam), the idea exists that the human mind is too limited to comprehend the full existential meaning of existence. Therefore, the divine power has helped mankind with special revelations, which can be found in the holy books, for there is essential knowledge that transcends the human mind. This thinking implies that to be fully connected with God, there is a moment when one believes and trusts that which cannot be proven or demonstrated by reasoning. In this religious way of making meaning, there may be a place where the dead are gathered and waiting to be reunited with the living. Unlike natural science, a discipline such as theology, based on the foundation of faith, cannot prove what is revealed by divine power but only demonstrate what is believed to be meaningful and reasonable.

The polarity between knowing and believing allows for many different spiritual beliefs. Most people in the Western Hemisphere take a position where knowledge and belief exist in a kind of tension with each other. Regardless of whether our meaning-making around loss and grief is based on knowing or believing, our way of approaching the uncertain and the spiritual questions will greatly influence our approach to grief. People can be open-minded and live their religion with a lot of inner space and flexibility, while others are strongly connected to the pole of faith and can even be dogmatic or fundamentalist. The same dogmatic or categorical approach can be said of people who lean on the pole of scientific knowledge, looking for scientific evidence for everything before trusting knowledge. The paradox, however, is that science can only actually develop when we as researchers dare to ask solid and open research questions and are open enough to learn that things can be different than we have always thought. If our research is only done to prove our existing beliefs, then knowledge will never be able to move beyond the beliefs of the individual researcher.

The same paradox applies to people who lean on faith. The more fixed our worldview is, the less open we are to reflecting on life's big questions. If the conviction is offered in religious or spiritual scriptures, we might not look for our own answers. The point is that if we rely solely on our knowledge or our faith, how will we be able to navigate the great paradoxes, tensions, and conflicting thoughts and feelings that we find within ourselves when we experience loss? Here, the IPM points out that the more we can live with open questions, the greater chance we have of finding our own answers and meaning structures. And the greater the chance that we can find a way to live with our grief in as meaningful a way as possible.

> It is when we can live with openness and wonder
> that we can live with the big questions in life
> and gradually live into our own answer.

Albert Einstein (1879–1955) was regarded by his peers and contemporaries as the greatest physicist of all time. Most people know him because he introduced the revolutionary theory of relativity and changed our entire scientific understanding of nature. Later in life, he also took pioneering steps in our understanding of quantum physics and even developed an interest in metaphysics. Einstein also spoke about the tension between faith and knowledge when he said:

> I am not an atheist . . . The human mind, no matter how highly trained, cannot grasp the universe. We are in the position of a little child, entering a huge library whose walls are covered to the ceiling with books in many different tongues. The child knows that someone must have written those books. It does not know who or how. It does not understand the languages in which they are written.
>
> (Einstein, 2000)

But on the other hand, Einstein said almost the same thing about science:

> One thing I have learned in a long life; that all our science, measured against reality, is primitive and childlike—yet it is the most precious thing we have. . . . We still do not know one thousandth of one percent of what nature has revealed to us. It is entirely possible that behind the perception of our senses, worlds are hidden of which we are unaware.
>
> (Einstein, 2000)

When we are confronted with the ultimate concern of meaninglessness, the existential tension between knowing and believing is activated, and here, openness is an important quality. It enables us to live with a framework of meaning that is not fixed or rigid but open to development. The spiritual dimension is about a spiritual quality through which we are open to a state of non-knowledge, which was also characteristic of humanity's great spiritual teachers (e.g. Meister Eckhardt, Rumi, Buddha). It may be associated with the quality of wonder in which we empty our minds of preconceptions and open ourselves to let the world speak to us. It is the emptiness that is open to receive and welcome the world as it is.

It puts the poles of knowledge and faith in a broader perspective
when dealing with the ultimate concern of meaninglessness
and asking oneself the question of whether one can have confidence in life
    again.

Text box 7.1   Existential reflection—significance

- What is the significance of the situation I find myself in?
- What do I believe in?
- How and why do I want to change the situation?
- Where do my strong urge and will come from?
- What does it tell me about what is significant in my life?
- Is there another way to approach the situation I am in?

Meaning and resonance

Experiencing a great loss is so contrary to what we understand as a just and meaningful world that our faith and beliefs can be temporarily completely disabled. The American psychologist Chrystal Park calls our different beliefs and assumptions about life and value sets "global meaning" (Park, 2013). During our life, we all build an assumption about how the world works, what is meaningful and worth living for, what is right and wrong, and many other beliefs. Most people hold on to this global meaning as a kind of framework for life without it necessarily being particularly explicit. It can pertain to a philosophy of life or a religion that contains ideas about what a person is, what existence is about, or what the meaning of life is. Such a framework can be called metaphysical or even moral. Often, it may even be a set of beliefs that we do not very often talk about or try to express, and perhaps we are not always aware of them as they become an ingrained part of the way we understand the world and life—right up until the moment they are challenged or threatened. When a great loss befalls us, this house of cards of "global meaning" can collapse around us. Now, we feel spiritually and existentially homeless.

It has been said that grief is homeless love.
But grief is much more than that;
it is an existential homelessness.
My assumptions have been shattered.
The world has become alien to me.

In this existential homelessness, our picture of the world has fallen apart, and we are working to feel at home in life again and find faith, trust, hope, and meaning. Therefore, the IPM describes the spiritual dimension in grief as a search for answers to the question: Can I believe in life again?

When our global meaning structure about life is broken down, we look to the small hopes or fragments of meaning structures that can be useful to find meaning in what is happening. For example, when we are affected by illness and have to give up functions and roles in life, we resort to concrete hopes for the future such as spending as much of our time as possible with the family, looking after a particular flower bed, or participating in a particular significant event. Meaning and hope are then placed in something concrete and manageable.

As long as life treats us well, most of us are not particularly aware of the structures of meaning that give our view of life a framework that helps us sustain life. You could even say that in our contemporary culture, it is not easy to become aware of and reflect on what is meaningful in our lives as long as we feel good. The pace of life in the wealthiest parts of the world has become so fast, and the amount of information, entertainment, and decisions pouring out at us are so enormous, that it makes it difficult to be aware of the connectedness to ourselves.

The German sociologist Hartmut Rosa (1965–) has analyzed this modern lifestyle and explains how in our accelerated world, we run the risk of becoming alienated from ourselves. In one of his books, Rosa gives the example of flying to a lovely vacation destination, being busy taking pictures and sharing them on social media, but not taking the time to really be where we are, take in the experience, digest it, and let it transform us (Rosa, 2020). Back home, we can say we were vacationing, but have we really been there, or did the trip end up being an exercise in collecting photographs and sharing them, even though no one really lets themselves be affected by it? Rosa's point is that our inner world can be understood as a unique space of resonance if we understand how to be in the world in a resonant way. Rosa describes resonance using four characteristics (Rosa, 2020):

First, there is an experience of being influenced. Something or someone touches us and does something to us. Being affected concerns our whole being in the world and all dimensions of our lives. When I listen to someone's story of grief, it resonates with my own stories. It activates something in me, and my bodily, emotional, and cognitive life is touched, as is the social, because it is a story that we now share the experience of. Being affected relates to the other person's effect on me.

Another characteristic is that I react to what happens. The story I hear calls for my response, and I respond based on the personal way I am affected. In my response, I reach out to the other person. I answer and enter into a real meeting, a dialogue, a conversation. In this way, I can offer my interior as a space where resonance can occur together with the other if I make sure to have a hospitable interior. I answer the call I hear in a personal way, even if it is in a professional context, by using my professional competences and skills in my own way. My personal life resonates in my answer.

The third characteristic is that this encounter has a transformative effect. I am touched, but the other is also touched. Rosa elaborates on this with the work of the German philosopher Hans-Georg Gadamer (1900–2002) and explains that in a genuine encounter, both my understanding horizon and the other person's horizon open up, and it can become a new shared horizon. This transformative effect, now inherent in this meeting or in our experiences, we can use to allow our personality to transform or change. This can be called maturation. Now, we are open to and aware of allowing our inner world to be further expanded, developed, and enriched. We come out of a real encounter differently than we went into it.

Finally, it is characteristic of resonance that there is no guarantee that it will succeed. As we have explained about moments of transcendence (Rosa, 2020), I can buy tickets to a concert or an exhibition with a great artist and open myself completely to enjoy it, but it may still happen that it will not be a truly transformative experience. Rosa calls it a volatility characteristic of resonance. We cannot produce or force experiences of resonance. When that happens, it is something extraordinary, a gift, just as it applies to many valuable experiences in life such as friendship, love, beauty, or even comfort after a loss. These are all resonant experiences that are a gift when they are there. But it is not something you can take for granted happens, nor can we conjure it up because we think we need it.

In the IPM, openness and resonance
are important to be able to find answers
to the question of
"How can I gain confidence in life again?"

Text box 7.2   Existential reflection—resonance

- When was the last time I was really affected or touched by something or someone?
- What did it do to me? How did I honor this experience?
- Did the experience stay with me and even transform me?
- What did this experience teach me about what is valuable in life?

Rituals

In Mexico, people celebrate *Dia de los Muertos*. In Bali cremation processions are common, and the mourners dress in colorful clothes and dance to show that they are happy that the deceased has gone to a better place. In many African cultures, people bury their dead family members in their private ground close to their house to keep their ancestors close so they can be asked for advice when needed.

Rituals are a symbolic or structured way of performing ceremonies or behaviors that can lead us through a time of transition and give form and expression to the transformation that takes place. At the core of these rituals is a sense of faith and trust, which is about the fact that I do not have to understand the world all by myself, but I have to be open to being helped along the way by connectedness to other people. As a human being, I am woven into a life-sustaining network of humans. The connection to this network takes place, among other things, through shared frameworks of meaning such as rituals. Examples of rituals associated with loss are divorce parties, funerals, grave visits, candle lighting, memorial exercises, and much more. When we have to navigate the existential tension between knowing and believing, between evidence and trust, between reason and faith, old frames of meaning and rituals can come in very useful.

Among the earliest rituals in life, apart from christening and naming, are rituals among Danish children to say goodbye to their nappy or pacifier. For example, in many places, there is a "pacifier tree," where the children hang their pacifiers on the tree in a ritual to say goodbye to the pacifier. The ritual is clearly about loss and transition, and it creates space for new meaning that helps to live with the loss of a physical object that has brought comfort. The preparation for the ritual and the larger perspective that all children hang the pacifier on the tree seems supportive and helpful. The symbolic act, ritual, or framework of shared meaning can help build a connection between people, and their shared experience can carry them through a difficult time. Rituals are frameworks of meaning that can open up a new way of being in the world and create new ways of experiencing our situation. In the Roman Catholic tradition, for example, there is the idea of the community of believers, which includes both the people who are alive and the people who have died. When you go to a Catholic service, you enter a ritualized space where the great divide between the living and the dead is temporarily revoked. Because God is greater than human life and death, and both the living and the dead are connected in God's creative all-encompassing love, the living and the dead are connected through God (Leget, 1997). And although the living do not have direct access to the loved ones they have lost to death, they have the opportunity to send their love and be connected in prayer to God. In this space, between knowing and believing, a path is opened to be together in the loss and grief and find words for a dimension that can hardly be understood.

> In the IPM, rituals form a frame and a transition
> to live without the lost.
> Symbolic actions build a bridge
> and open up new ways for life to go on.

Many mourning rituals provide answers to where the dead should be kept or how to get in touch with them. This may be an indication that it is a completely biologically based need to understand where our loved ones are (O'Connor, 2022). In the wake of loss, we often show an overwhelming urge to reach for what we have lost, to find a way back to it, or perhaps even to look for meaning in the meaninglessness. The world's religions have long answered our desire to find what we have lost or connect with our deceased. For example, we turn toward a religious belief to understand the meaning of life and a deceased person's place in the universe because religions offer answers that can soothe and comfort the grieving (O'Connor, 2022). However, not all rituals are situated in a religious belief.

Text box 7.3   Spiritual reflection—where are they now?

- Where are they now?
- Will I see them again?
- Is there a way to be in touch with what I have lost?
- Is there a form of being that is nonbeing?
- How do I keep the dead alive?
- Which rituals can create a connectedness?

Loss as a window to existential values

In his classical work Faust, the German polymath and writer Johann Wolfgang von Goethe (1749–1832) compares the human mind with a weaving loom. The incredible velocity of the human mind when connecting thoughts and associations is compared to the way one treadle of a loom can knit together an infinite number of threads, producing a weaver's masterpiece (von Goethe, 1808/1988).

Meaningful connections to life, a job, a cause, other people, nature, art can be the structure of a meaningful and happy life. When these connections are broken, it has a huge effect on our well-being. When we lose something or someone we care about, the world can become completely dark. From a spiritual perspective, the meaning and purpose of our lives seem to have disappeared. We cannot understand a great loss all at once. And sometimes, we do not even see the point of living. In such situations, it is as if all four of the ultimate concerns collapse at once, showing how interconnected they are.

> When everything becomes meaningless,
> there is no meaning in the freedom to choose,
> we feel isolated from the rest of humanity,
> and we may not even mind that one day, we die.

Although the meaninglessness at the first blow of a loss can confront us with complete darkness, as our eyes adjust to the darkness, we can begin to discern small glimmers of light. In this sense, van Gogh's painting of the starry night mentioned at the beginning of the chapter has another interesting meaning. Although the stars in the sky shine all day long, we only begin to notice them when the sun sets and evening falls. We need the dark so we can see the light of the stars or, in the north, maybe even a beautiful aurora. Similarly, existential values may become clearer after a loss. Existential values can be compared to stars, because often, we are not aware of them or need to be aware of them to find our way in daily life.

> It is in the darkness after a loss
> that we can suddenly see the stars in the sky.
> It is the same with our existential values.
> It is after a loss that we become aware of them,
> so they can help us with orientation
> and making choices.

It is a characteristic of values that they are not concrete and tangible. Fairness, honesty, integrity, trust, sincerity: we have an idea about what they are, they point in a certain direction, but it is difficult to fully grasp or define them. And yet if we think about our lives, we discover that we often use them to inform us about our daily choices and lifestyle. They help set our inner compass in situations in which we are in doubt or confused about the right decision. They can give us a sense of direction, purpose, and meaning in life.

When we are in grief, we can experience that the house of global meaning we had built, which gave us existential security and meaning, is collapsing. Now, we feel that we have become existentially homeless and are fully exposed to the ultimate concern of meaninglessness. The power of loss and grief is that they open up the world as we know it and open up the existential dimension of life. There is nothing beautiful about being in the cold and darkness of existential homelessness. And yet it is the place where we begin to see stars and maybe even a bright aurora, and now, in the dark, we come into contact with the reality that the world is bigger than we thought, and we look for clearer existential values that can now be our guiding stars.

Text box 7.4   Existential reflection—your inner space

Close your eyes and turn your attention inward to your inner life. What picture do you get of your inner life? Is it a large and open landscape such as the Grand Canyon in the USA? Is it a fenced garden with beautiful flowers and fountains like in Spain? Is it an interior cathedral with the grandeur of Chartres Cathedral in France? Or a completely different picture? Stay with the image and investigate if it is a good place to be. What do you come into contact with? What do you miss? How can this place help you connect to your inner strength?

Living the question: Can I believe in life again?

Our mind creates meaning in everything we see or perceive. This is also the case when we encounter unexpected opposition in life such as loss and grief. We try to give it meaning and put it into a greater understanding and meaning in life to avoid the anxiety of a life without structure and purpose. If we cannot find a greater explanation or meaning in it, we feel powerless and lose trust and faith. When we discover meaning, we use it as a structure around which we can build our understandings and values. This now becomes our safety net because now, there is a basis for creating more meaning when we understand our world and can live according to our values. If this value is, for example, helping others, then we start to find ways to do that or create a working life that is about helping others. Everything we do is now measured against the meaningfulness of helping others. It dictates our values and how we live our lives. Viktor Frankl would say that true meaning and happiness are found when meaning and value extend beyond ourselves (Frankl, 1946/2006). How can we help the other person find it? How do we provide existential support that is helpful in the wake of loss and grief? Frankl has an example of an existential conversation with a patient:

"Patient: But this inner turmoil . . .

Frankl: Don't watch your inner turmoil, but turn your gaze to what is waiting for you. What counts is not what lurks in the depths, but what waits in the future, waits to be actualized by you."

(Frankl, 1967)

Frankl helps his patient find meaning. Perhaps he even helped this person to see patterns and experiences that make up a whole and that help to find themselves and get in touch with what is important right now.

One cannot find meaning that applies once and for all
and which can act as a response throughout a lifetime.
Meanings change, and therefore, the meaning of life changes.
Finding meaning is a continuous quest for us.

The question of meaning is not a question we can answer once and for all. In the IPM, it is pointed out that we can live the question in each and every loss we have. This means that we must live in the paradoxes of life. For example, only by experiencing meaninglessness can we become aware and discover our meaning. By understanding and living with the paradox, I can answer it anew after a loss.

"So what am I supposed to do?" a doctor asked during one of our lectures in a group of healthcare professionals. "With the limited time I have available, what would you like me to say to the patient to make him feel better?" It is a question we have been asked many times when we at the Center for Grief and Existential Values work with healthcare staff or volunteers on how to provide existential care. Usually, these lectures are about the big questions of life and how they are brought to the fore when we suffer a loss. The desire to alleviate suffering is admirable, and when it is about our own losses, it is natural that we want to find a way. It is also quite important that we dare to offer this conversation to each other. But providing existential care to yourself or others, like reflecting on the big questions in life, is not an exact science or a matter of using specific magic words that will do the trick. Human communication in general and existential communication in particular is complex and involves layers of meaning in the conversation that cannot be reduced to a formula. We might seek three magic questions or three phrases for the relief of existential suffering, but that would be like giving someone who wants to talk to people from Japan the three most common phrases used in the Japanese language and then claim that now, this person is able to speak Japanese.

Rather, as we learned in relation to the emotional dimension, part of the process is being patient and enduring the meaninglessness and giving it some space, while at the same time, we have to take responsibility for the process and make sure that we are open and hospitable so that new resonance can arise in the meeting. Admittedly, it can be a complex state when suffering, but like any other skill, it can be learned through training and attention. It is like learning a new language. It gets easier if we practice every day without being too focused on seeing progress. If you feel discouraged about learning the art of existential conversation, remember that the key to this particular language is already within you, because you are a human being just like every other human being, and you probably already use many of the words in this language. You just have to learn to put them together in a way that reflects and opens an existential mindset. It is about a way of thinking and a state of mind that looks for meeting the other person in a shared vulnerability of struggling with the ultimate concerns we all struggle with: death, freedom, aloneness, and meaninglessness. Developing the art of existential conversation is based on existentially maturing as a human being. It asks for the development of inner space to meet the big questions in life. As Rilke said: "You must live the questions" (Rilke, 2000). In order to be able to reflect alone or together with another human being on the great fundamental questions of life, we need to be aware of our own presence and our own reflections. It is about daring to ask and learning to live with the right questions more than having or giving the right answers.

Living the existential questions is the understanding
that we all share the vulnerability of loss with each other,
and we all search for meaning and authenticity
when life is hard.

The important thing is to be open to reflecting the big questions and not shy away from a conversation about loss and grief. Have the courage to go to the inner dialogue or a conversation with an awareness that grief opens a space into the existential tensions and paradoxes of life. It can probably help the other person if we are aware that we are facing life's big questions and that there are no right or wrong answers here, only more or less personal and authentic ways to answer.

Text box 7.5   Existential reflection—how do you live the existential questions?

- How do you live the existential questions? Is it something you take the time for? Have you built some moments of reflection into your life?
- How do you bring the existential dimension of life into your work? Is there an integration of who you are in your work and who you are as a private person from an existential perspective?
- Which one of the four ultimate concerns is your biggest struggle? What is your strategy to avoid being confronted with it? How does it affect your awareness of the other ultimate concerns?
- How do you help other people to find their own answers to the ultimate concerns of death, freedom, isolation, and meaninglessness?

When we are teaching about loss, grief, and existence, we always ask participants what they need when they are grieving. Often, they answer something along the lines that they would need a nonjudgmental person to listen, experience recognition of the loss, and compassion from others, a warm hug from a friend, but not too much advice. All of these things are important. However, what most often characterizes these answers is that we completely overlook grief as a sovereign expression of life or grief as sacred ground for the individual. An answer could also be "Someone who can compassionately remind me who I am."

The IPM suggests that existential care
means getting in touch with who I am.
This means that when we are in danger of succumbing to the pain of our loss,
the real support is to be helped into the connectedness with myself
and, from here, find my authentic answer to the situation.

Every person who grieves tries to give meaning to the experiences and seeks to be themselves in the way they express their grief. Finding out who I am when grieving is a process that takes time. When we enter into this process, it helps that a space can be opened in which self-reflection is welcomed. This can happen through resonant and transcendent encounters with nature or art. Or we get there via yoga or dance or a meeting with another human being in which a space is opened to examine the existential questions.

The IPM points out that in grief, the help lies in
creating a space where we can meet ourselves.
This space can be created professionally
but also in friendships, love, nature, and aesthetics.

In this space, we have the opportunity to find ourselves when we are in grief, and in time, perhaps, find a new point of view or new meaning. However, it requires that the existential conversation resonates with new meaning. As Hartmut Rosa (2020) describes resonance, it is not a given that it will happen, but if we are open to being affected and we can allow transcendent experiences, then we can be aware of how the meeting resonates in our own personal lives and answer the call by seeing the gift it is that now, something extraordinary is happening to me.

Text box 7.6   Existential reflection—existential awareness

- Do you know how you reflect on life's big questions?
- What basic existential challenges are dominant in your life?
- Are you aware of your own losses and how they have affected your outlook on life?
- Are you aware of how your own view of loss and existence affects the way you provide care?

Hardly anyone with a brush and canvas can paint like van Gogh, and few people with an electric guitar can play like Jimi Hendrix. Mastering an art is a process that requires time, effort, and potential. It takes practice to try and fail many times before you succeed. Understanding and reflecting on life's big questions is a lifelong process. Although this book has explained the basic elements of an existential approach to loss and grief and the integrative understanding of the IPM, unlike playing music, there is no composition we can follow that will guarantee that the piece of music sounds good. Alleviating one's own or another's pain in grief is similar to improvising in music. Once one has acquired the skills to play an instrument and there is a sense of musicality, improvisation can become an encounter in which something new can happen. It is in this improvisation that the space is opened in which we can think about the question of whether we can believe in life again. Then, changes will start happening.

Personal meaning, authenticity, and spiritual awareness are lifelong challenges for all of us. When we experience loss and grief, our spiritual development also plays a role in the awareness, understanding, and approach to what is happening. If we want to help ourselves or others to increase awareness of the spiritual approach to grief, it requires increased awareness of the existential tensions and the spiritual dimension. If we are aware of our own existential balances and we live life's big questions ourselves, we are better able to enter into a space in which reflections on existential tensions are taken up. In the following exercise, you are invited to look at the history of your own spiritual development.

Text box 7.7   Existential reflection on spiritual development

Take a piece of paper and draw a line from your birth to today. Think back to when you were young and remember how you grew up around people who taught you a certain way of looking at life. It can be in a religious community or church but also the family you were born into, the people who raised you, the teachers at school, your peers and friends. Try to recover an image of the worldview you had in the first ten years of your life. From there, try to reconstruct your spiritual development. In most people's lives, there are continuity and discontinuity, transformation and development, doubt and existential immersion. Whenever there has been a major change or decisive break, there will likely have been changes in your worldview as well. In this way, try to mark how your inner life, your spiritual development, has taken shape during your life. In what follows, we offer some questions for reflection on the development of your worldview, your beliefs, and the attribution of meaning so that you can reconstruct the history of your own spiritual development.

- What were your sources of meaning when you were growing up?
- What religious or spiritual belief were you influenced by as a child?
- Who or what has inspired you along the way in your spiritual development?
- Are there certain experiences that have changed your spiritual development?
- Do you have a life philosophy or a motto in life that you live by?
- Which ritual or part of your everyday life is most important to you? Has it changed during your life? What has influenced this daily ritual?
- Are there certain books or thinkers that have influenced your way of understanding life?
- What are you longing for in life? What makes you angry in life?
- What sources do you draw on for inner strength?
- What inspires you?
- What existential values do you have?

The transformative potential of finding meaning

After a great loss in life, we can discover that both existential poles of "knowing" and "believing" have collapsed. The security of a scientific worldview is not of much help when we are confronted with the meaninglessness of life. And the security of a religious worldview may not be comforting if it feels as if you have been abandoned by God. In fact, this experience of complete abandonment, emptiness, and desolation is at the heart of the Christian tradition. When Jesus died on the cross, he was not only betrayed by one of his friends, abandoned by his disciples, unjustly judged, and rejected by the masses; his last words also expressed his experience of the absence of God. "The dark night of the soul" is what it is called in the Christian mystical tradition, which alludes to an absolute dark night of meaninglessness in which nothing is left and no religious faith can offer any comfort.

This chapter has focused on navigating the existential tension between meaning and meaninglessness in the IPM. Loss and grief can be devastating and bring us to the bare ground or the desert in human existence.

It is when our frameworks of meaning have been broken down
that we experience the greatest meaninglessness.
A last resort might be to look for a connectedness in our inner self
to discover sparks of light, meaning, or longing
that can guide us back to the world of the living and reconnect us with life.

Although paradoxical, it is only by accepting our meaninglessness that we can open ourselves to the possibility of life speaking to us. Ultimately, it is natural for every living being to seek self-preservation and its own well-being. You might even say that it is a good thing to take responsibility for our own happiness and strive to flourish in such a way that we have a fulfilling life. However, it can become problematic when this is done in a way that avoids confronting the ultimate concerns of death, freedom, loneliness, and meaninglessness.

The American psychologist Abraham Maslow (1908–1970) already in 1943 described the central human needs inserted in a pyramid, where physical needs are at the bottom, the feeling of belonging and being connected is located in the middle of the pyramid, and at the top, Maslow put the need for self-realization, i.e., to seek one's own happiness.

What may be less known is
that in 1968,
Maslow added an extra dimension to his pyramid of basic human needs
and described that humans also naturally seek transcendence.
(Maslow, 1968/2013)

Transcendence is, in other words, the experience of being able to see things in a larger perspective, being able to transcend oneself and one's own worries. If we try to avoid confronting life's big questions by seeking reassurance and pretending there is a way to live a meaningful and fulfilling life without dealing with life's big questions, talking to others about loss and grief, or avoiding confronting ourselves with the suffering, then we close off the resonance this can offer and, thus, our personal development. Then when we suffer a loss, there is nothing to learn, because we consider a loss to be nothing but a loss. Although we may try to repair the loss or blur its meaning, it is mostly self-preservation because we are not looking for what this loss tells us about life. Now, we run the risk of starting to ruminate, practice magical thinking, and other reactions that keep our consciousness in a loop that does not shift our understanding and behavior. It becomes a kind of self-perpetuating attitude toward life that does not transform, a self-inflicted torment.

According to the great spiritual traditions, the way out of this self-righteous attitude to life, which ends up being a self-inflicted prison, is only possible when we can evolve from a self-preserving self to a decentered self. A decentered self means that we have discovered that we are not the center of the world and that the primary goal in life is not self-preservation. In the same way as Rabindranath Tagore's image at the beginning of the chapter of planting a tree, knowing that you yourself will not sit in its shade. Or perhaps, as many parents think, that their children's lives are more important than their own. The great religious traditions of the world are a school of life for this transformation from self-preservation to decentering. The Jewish, Christian, and Muslim traditions teach us that when we live from a transcendent connectedness with God, who is the center of the universe, we discover an inner freedom because we discover that life is not only about us and that the responsibility for all evil of the world does not rest on our shoulders. From this perspective, loss and grief are a chance to break out of our self-centered existence. Our losses are painful and not self-chosen, but they confront us with our greatest fears and anxieties, the ultimate limitations of our existence, and help us see the limits of our own control and will. The big question, however, is whether we try to numb or avoid the pain or whether we can also see this pain as a kind of birth pain, like labor that will result in a different life. Naturally, it should not sound heroic, because there is nothing romantic about it, and we are constantly reminded that we have to struggle with the idea that we did not want the loss and therefore cannot take responsibility for our reaction. Accepting the pain takes courage, and it is also hard work, just like any natural birthing process is.

The transformation process from a self-sustaining to a decentralized self has its own pitfalls. The connection to God or fellow human beings can be a new way to numb the pain and avoid facing the ultimate concerns. In the language of the spiritual traditions, this would be phrased as moving away from the transcendence of a divine presence and creating one's own image of God. Real connectedness to the divine or the transcendent involves an openness to the divine. The divine mystery is greater than we can comprehend with our thoughts and express with our words. Just as resonance can only happen if we dare to be open to it, we can allow transcendent experiences that can transform us. In such encounters, we can look for our own answers and our own authenticity. You can call that regaining confidence in life again. The central issue in this dimension of new confidence in life cannot be achieved by willpower. It cannot even be pursued directly; as Rilke eloquently pointed out in his advice, we have to "live the questions."

In the IPM, finding new confidence in life is the fruit of a process
in which the question is lived
while we are open to resonance
as we search for our own meaning, authenticity, and transcendence.

Central points in Chapter 7

- The spiritual dimension in the IPM is the dimension in which we respond to our loss and grief by seeking meaning, faith, hope, trust, resonance, and transcendence.
- When art reaches out to us and we are touched in a deeply personal way, art has the potential to connect us more deeply with aspects of ourselves that we might not have been in touch with.
- Spirituality is the dynamic dimension of human life that relates to the way people (individual and society) experience, express, and/or seek meaning, purpose, and transcendence and the way they connect to the moment, to themselves, to others, to nature, to the significant and/or the sacred.
- In the spiritual dimension of the IPM, we navigate the existential tension between meaninglessness and meaning by combining thoughts and feelings on a continuum between knowing and believing.
- It has been said that grief is homeless love. But grief is much more than that; it is existential homelessness. The world has become alien to me.
- Our interior can be understood as a unique space of resonance if we understand how to be in the world in a resonant way.
- Rituals are a symbolic or structured way of performing ceremonies or actions that can lead us through a time of transition and give form and expression to the change that is taking place.
- One cannot find meaning that applies once and for all and that will serve as an answer throughout a lifetime. Meanings change, and therefore, the meaning of life changes. Therefore, the question of meaning is not one we can answer once and for all.
- When our frameworks of meaning are put out of action, we experience the greatest meaninglessness. A way out may be to look for connectedness within ourselves, thereby searching for sparks of light, meaning, or longing that can guide us back to connectedness with ourselves and life again.

Interlude: Ann's struggle with the spiritual dimension of loss

As Ann opened up to feeling her deep longing for connectedness and intimacy, she began to suffer from feelings of deep loneliness and sadness. It hurt to feel alone, like she was isolated from the rest of humanity or excluded from something that others had. Even after all she had accomplished in life, she felt a deep sense of meaninglessness that she had not felt before. She knew it was part of her life story and who she was. Maybe she would never get rid of it completely, but perhaps she could get better at living with it. It became clear to her that avoiding thinking about her parents or her background did not help, but the sense of loss put her in touch with a part of herself that she had forgotten. She had not previously noticed how overwhelming her work ambitions had been and how they had given her a sense of meaning in life. But now, she could also see that these ambitions had suppressed many other aspects of herself. Ann gradually realized that her body had given her a wake-up call and that she would have to accept the deep wounds of her early youth while integrating new ways of connecting with people if she was to find a sense of meaning and hope in life again. It would also involve finding new meaningful goals in life alongside work-related recognition and rewards. She actually had the experience that the yoga training gave her a new sense of well-being and the breathing exercises helped her with being in the moment. She also thought more about how she wanted to work less and pursue her own activities instead of waiting with leisure activities until she was retired.

In the Center for Grief and Existential Values, we suggested reflecting on how to find meaning by getting more in touch with her passion in life. It turned out that she had always been passionate about a little local gallery for amateur artists. She had always thought that she contributed to society by paying a lot of taxes on her personal income, but now, it made more sense for her to contribute by working as a volunteer in this little art gallery. It was a good process to choose this particular place to volunteer, because it gave her a whole new sense of accomplishment and satisfaction that extended beyond herself and her own needs. It gave her a sense of resonance and being part of something bigger. In a way, it made her feel a kind of transcendence and gave her a sense of belonging in her community.

Chapter 8

Living our loss

One day when I was painting,
I suddenly discovered that the black color had invaded the entire canvas.
There was no shape, no contrast, no transparency.
In this extreme,
I suddenly began to see the negation of the black.
Out of the darkness a clarity emerged.
My instrument was no longer the black,
but this mysterious light
that comes from the darkness.

Freely after Pierre Soulages (2014)

Pierre Soulages (1919–2022) was a French painter who became known for his thick black-brushstroke paintings labeled *outrenoir* ("beyond black"). While his paintings are characterized by abstractions based on the black lines on light backgrounds, his vision with the black paintings was to capture the reflection of the void and the emptiness that we put in it. It has been described as a harmonic explosion beyond the religious; it is the tensions of emptiness and fullness, strength, and vulnerability. "The absence of light is already quite moving," Soulages explained. "When we see a painting on a wall, it's a window, . . . A window looks outside, but a painting should do the opposite—it should look inside of us" (Soulages, 2014).

The ability to live with one's losses is the ability
to become aware of, to turn toward, and to engage in these losses
with the aim of carrying them with us and learning from them.

DOI: 10.4324/9781003499060-8

Perhaps our losses work like Pierre Soulages's "beyond black" paintings; they become a window to look into ourselves. Like any ability, to look through this window is not something we just possess by nature. We have to train ourselves in it through practice. Loss is like life: searching for a meaningful way to live is both an adventure and a struggle. Existentialist thinkers have proposed that we are always searching for existential meaning in life on the way to becoming ourselves and living authentically. This is also expressed in the book *Top Five Regrets of the Dying* by hospice nurse Bronnie Ware (Ware, 2011/2019). She describes that what most people wish when they die is that they had lived their lives with the courage to be true to themselves.

> Speaking of losses, it could mean
> that we develop the courage to dare to look at our losses,
> facing the pain, honoring the loss, and expressing grief meaningfully,
> thereby being true to ourselves and showing who we are.

As life moves along, we may not ask ourselves how we want to live, because as long as things are working, there may not be much reason to question the state of affairs. But when we are confronted with loss or death, we experience an existential void, and then we begin to question the meaning of our lives, and we begin to search for existential meaning and content in life. Our loss can act as a stumbling block for our inner self to be free. In this book, we have described why and how the IPM sees our losses not only as obstacles but also as openings to consider our existential meaning and values by looking for a deeper connectedness with ourselves. In other words, grief is not only loss and pain but also a potential for increased existential awareness.

> The IPM is not giving answers to how we should grieve.
> The model is about understanding that grief opens a space
> in which we are invited to look at the existential tensions and paradoxes
>   in life.
> There are no right or wrong answers in this
> but more or less authentic ways
> to answer life's ultimate concerns of
> death, loneliness, freedom, responsibility, and meaninglessness.

The basic understanding in the IPM is that loss and grief cannot be avoided. Loss is a natural and common human condition that confronts us with the ultimate limitation of human existence. This book has shown that living with one's losses means living the ultimate concerns of life that we all face when grieving and balancing the basic existential tensions that open up to us after a loss. The challenge is not to avoid grief and not to neglect the pain, minimize it, or look for ways that let us put it aside as quickly as possible. On the contrary. Grief has an ethical demand to us: it is a supreme expression of love for what has been lost and thus an expression of who we are. When we search for what is a meaningful way for us to express grief, we can approach an authentic expression of what is meaningful and important in our lives, and it is in this expression that we find a way to live with our grief.

The IPM points out that grief is closely connected to what we love, but it is also closely connected to who we are, our authenticity, and to our meaning and values in life. Therefore, we feel an urge to explore these aspects of life while grieving. It also means that no one can tell us what the right size is for our grief or what the right way is to grieve. In the IPM, the understanding is that our grief never completely goes away; rather, it stays with us to help us feel the connectedness, coherence, and resonance of our existence.

> The IPM invites us to explore what is a meaningful way for us to grieve
> and express our connectedness to the lost
> so we feel we are honoring the love and meaningfulness in our lives.

Suffering without meaning leads to despair, but suffering as a search for meaning and values holds the potential to live one's life the way we want. The IPM points to how loss and suffering can lead to more connectedness and more authenticity.

> We are living with our loss
> when we are able to connect with our loss,
> when we have the courage to feel the suffering it causes
> and get in touch with the quest for existential meaning that arises
> and thus also see the possibility of finding our own authenticity.

As many of the existentialist thinkers mentioned in this book have pointed out, the search for existential meaning will often feel like a powerful force within us, and we have the choice of either becoming afraid of the questions that now come from within us or finding the courage to answer the pressure from within. In the IPM, this is taken a step further by pointing out that taking responsibility for finding the balances in our grief can help us move into a greater existential awareness, more authenticity, freedom, and flexibility to live our lives as we wish despite our loss. The idea of the IPM is not that we will experience more happiness as a result of daring to deal with our grief. But if we dare to feel our grief, we develop more existential awareness, which enables us to experience more intense satisfaction and inner peace, because now, we can use our understanding of existential meaning as a compass.

Based on the ideas in this book, the IPM first of all points out that we must recognize all losses in life, not just losses as a result of death, when a close person dies. As philosopher Will Durant paraphrased the ancient Greek philosopher Aristotle, "We are what we repeatedly do . . . therefore excellence is not an act, but a habit" (Durant, 1926).

> Imagine that we could erect little tombstones in our mind
> to mark all our losses and their meaning.
> Then, we could learn from each loss we experience
> and not only from the losses that are related to death.

And this could be even better if we could also learn to see and be aware of others' losses along the way and recognize and show compassion for all the losses we all have as human beings. In this way, we would train our grief muscle and be better prepared for the central losses we encounter in life. We would be better at talking with each other about our inner pain, because we would not be so unfamiliar with the pain loss inflicts on us. We could even stop discussing how many different losses there are or whose losses are the most painful and which losses deserve the most compassion and support from others.

> We could start talking about how loss, grief, and suffering
> unite us in our humanity and vulnerability.
> Then, the loss ignites a search for a life in which we recognize our
>   connectedness
> and which is worth living in spite of the suffering and because of the suffering.

Throughout the book, the IPM points out that we can live with our losses when we recognize that they open a space for the ultimate questions of human life, and we try to balance the existential tensions that arise. The IPM does not propose achieving a specific goal after a significant loss or providing the answers to how any of us can live with our loss. Rather, the model is about each of us becoming aware of our grief, becoming aware of how we want to grieve, finding our own meaning and resonance in life with grief so that our expression of life becomes as authentic as possible.

On the journey there, it is important how we balance our basic concerns and answer to the existential tensions in life. It raises a series of monuments of meaningful moments along the way that become the essence of our lives.

Our loss aversion gets in the way

The Nobel Prize winner, bestselling author, and psychologist Daniel Kahneman writes in the book *Thinking—Fast and Slow* about loss aversion (Kahneman, 2012). In researching financial losses, Kahneman discovered that we generally find losses to be twice as potent as gains. This means that we tend to regard losses as much more powerful than what we can gain from the loss, and we place more importance on what we have lost than what we gained before or even after the loss. This illustrates that loss aversion can play a dominant role in decision-making if we want to avoid losses more than we look for the gains that might result. This is probably because we intuitively have an understanding of how painful loss can be.

We do not actually know if the concept of loss aversion applies to contexts other than economics, where it has been demonstrated, but researchers generally consider loss aversion to be both irrational and something that controls our minds. It is likely that for most of us, the fear of death and loss is something that gets in the way of us living life freely. This can also affect the way we evaluate our losses if we focus on what has been lost and are reluctant to look for or talk about the gains that the loss also paved the way for. If we imagine the suffering of grief as a continuum, then gain or growth may not be at the opposite end of loss. Rather, if we dare to look at it, suffering and pain can be considered to coincide with gain and growth.

This means that when we grieve,
we must dare to not only look for the absence of suffering
but also for what new understanding of life arises from our loss.

We may be reluctant to talk about it when something good came from the loss because we then feel we are not grieving enough or sufficiently honoring what was lost. But in the IPM, loss and gain go hand in hand, so here, it is really about having the courage to acknowledge the presence of both.

Text box 8.1   Existential reflection—the gain of loss

- What have I learned from this loss in my life?
- What have I found out about the love I had for the lost?
- What new opportunities does this loss open up to me?
- What do I hope for now?
- How can I seek love and connectedness even though I now know I might lose them again?

Loss aversion can also affect how we talk about our losses and seek coherence in them. If you are currently close to someone with a significant loss, you may be reluctant to talk about this aspect of loss because loss aversion gets in the way of developing a common language about loss and grief. Loss aversion can also prevent us from looking at how loss affects us and how we can learn from loss. It is as if our mind creates a contradictory relationship between loss and gain because grief is so devilishly painful, and therefore, we naturally try to avoid loss and fail to look at it. But life shrinks and expands in proportion to our courage. Most of our losses happen because they are inevitable, and even if we wish they had not happened or that we could prevent them, not talking about them does not change this. The problem is that if we do not have the courage to talk about our losses or look at them, then we miss the opportunity to honor them and let them help us into a balance. It is through communication and community that we can regain flexibility in our consciousness, and from here, we can learn to live with them. If we can find a way to be in touch with our loss, then we can begin to see similarities in our existential learning and perhaps even experience existential growth.

Loss can turn into growth

In the Danish novel *Lucky Per* by the Nobel Prize–winning author Henrik Pontoppidan (1857–1943), the gifted protagonist Per is forced to give up his career at the height of his success (Pontoppidan, 1904/2019). Per Sidenius is the son of a strict priest from the countryside who lives under frugal, religious conditions. His dream of success forces Per to confront the limitations of his family heritage and social background to go to Copenhagen and become an engineer. In doing so, he breaks all ties to his family and his former life. In this metamorphosis, Per devises a large and prestigious engineering project. But as he works to get it funded, Per's own inability to compromise ends up getting in his way, and his dreams come crashing down. Per withdraws from the busy scene of Copenhagen and ends up pursuing his own personal happiness back in his old neighborhood, where he lives in ascetic absorption as a civil servant in the countryside. A main theme in this story is the relationship between fortune and happiness, as the Danish word "lykke" can mean both. While Per initially views happiness as a result of success and achievement, he eventually realizes through all his losses that happiness can be achieved independently of worldly success.

Some critics consider *Lucky Per* to be one of the greatest Danish novels of all time. The book was made into a movie in 2018. In the book, the loss of worldly success is understood not as defeat but as a victory over the circumstances that are generally defined as success. An existentialist would say that Per loses his dreams, his goals, his flexibility, his outlook on life, but he regains his freedom. Per ends up living authentically, which is the real happiness of his life. The very capacity of being uncompromising that helps him get ahead in the world also becomes his shortfall and emptiness, because he apparently does not manage to create enough balance in it. This is also reflected in his marriage. In the book, Per is sent several times on a personal quest to find existential meaning through his losses and to explore his values and his way of living in light of these losses.

Many philosophers and researchers have been concerned with the question of whether loss spurs growth. After we have suffered a loss and we have struggled to live with the grief, it becomes clear that life will never be the same again.

> We would like to believe that the grief slowly becomes less and less with time, but it is probably more likely
> that we readjust, integrate the loss, and grow with the grief.

This may feel like our grief is lessening, but since the love does not change, the grief itself most likely will not change either, even if the acute reactions go away.

> It is probably rather the case that the more integrated the loss is in us and our lives,
> the fewer existential imbalances we will experience from it.

It naturally alleviates the entire complex experience of grief. But one of the most common misconceptions about grief remains that it will subside over time as we adjust to living with the loss. However, there is a fundamental difference in whether it is the shock and acute grief that subsides or whether it is the love for the lost that subsides. Precisely for this reason, grief can be seen as a new form of love that arises after a great loss. Grief is born out of the love we have for what we lost and deeply miss, and therefore, it is a testimony to how much we love. After the loss, however, the grief must now include a new expression of love, a love that overcomes death.

Grief researcher Lois Tonkin wrote an article in 1996 about how we grow around our grief, which is a way of healing after grief (Tonkin, 1996). In Figure 8.1, this is depicted as a learning process, in the understanding that we develop with our grief and gradually learn to endure it and live with it.

The idea that major life crises can result in positive change has also been described as *posttraumatic growth*. Although very old, the idea that adversity spurs growth was taken up by researchers Tedeschi and Calhoun, who structured research on this topic more than 20 years ago (Tedeschi & Calhoun, 1996, 2008). Tedeschi and Calhoun introduced a model of how emotional disequilibrium, fractured narratives, and shattered assumptions redirect our thinking and revise our understanding of the world. Based on their research, it is shown that for most people, major difficulties in life lead to increased personal strength, closer relationships, greater appreciation of life, the search for new opportunities, and also

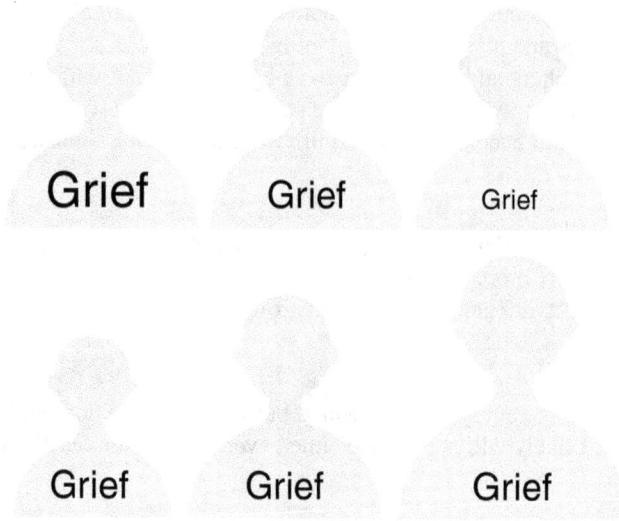

Figure 8.1 Growth model of grief (Guldin, 2018) depicting that grief does not diminish over time, but we can grow, which makes grief look smaller.

spiritual development. Although these types of growth in maturity and strength did not happen overnight, they could demonstrate a gradual development over a period of years following a loss.

In one of our own studies on trajectories of grief in Denmark, we asked the respondents about their posttraumatic growth. More than a thousand people responded with what they had taken with them from the loss and reported many different kinds of learning back to us. For example, "I have developed a new understanding of life"; "We have developed a new closeness in our family and support each other more"; "I have less anxiety, because I have stared my worst fear in the eye, and now I know that I will manage no matter what" (Guldin, 2019). It is important to emphasize that these words were not written right after the loss but at least a year and a half after their loss. Let us look at the personal growth expressed by these grievers. It is most often expressed as learning new aspects about themselves, their character, and personal strengths, as increased relational knowledge, or as existential learning about life, death, loneliness, or meaning.

Posttraumatic growth is sometimes understood as an aspect of positive psychology or a cultural ideal of being able to turn adversity into growth and development if we are strong enough to do so. However, posttraumatic growth is not developed in this light but rather to be able to look at the whole experience of loss and not just the negative or painful aspects. If you look at the research on growth after loss, it also turns out that the vast majority of people have the experience of learning new aspects about their existence while being challenged by grief.

> Naturally, science should be interested in looking at the learning process as an important aspect of grief more than as an ideal or end in itself.
> Loss and grief, like love, are identity-creating forces.

If you think about it, it is perhaps not so strange that we change and learn during the grief process, since it is also generally accepted that love changes us and that we learn from it. It opens our hearts and our minds. If the same is true of grief, why should grief not change us?

The experience of growth or learning is perhaps more unlikely to emerge if it is turned into a goal we need to achieve.

> The IPM carries forward the idea that the experience of learning or growth is more likely to be part of the process
> if we are looking for ways to live with the grief.
> But the IPM differs significantly from previous models of grief,
> because it does not point to a specific goal for the grief process
> but rather to the paradox that loss can turn into growth
> if we are open to living the questions of our existence.

The experience of growth will hardly feel authentic if researchers or other people can define what growth should look like, because then, chances are that it feels more limiting than enriching. Moreover, how can growth possibly look the same in very different people of different ages, life trajectories, and maturity? Existentially, growth is more likely to occur in a natural developmental process of a person moving toward becoming themselves in an innate search for authenticity.

The transformative potential of loss

In the IPM, it is considered a paradox that the very same forces that give us suffering and pain are the same that initiate change and growth. This has also been called *the paradoxical theory of change* (Beisser, 1970). The paradoxical theory of change is a theory of how suffering is an agent of change, but acceptance is a prerequisite for us to create change. For example, we can spend a lot of energy fighting the grief and looking at the loss, which prevents us from integrating the loss into our lives and adapting to the changes. The theory explains that the moment we accept the loss, we can begin to look at it, and this will set off a process of change.

One day, we in the Center for Grief and Existential Values were out giving a lecture to a group of parents who had the heart-wrenching grief of their child struggling with mental problems. We told them about the paradoxical theory of change, and one parent raised his hand. He had a son with a neurological disease and said, "I just do not feel right about seeking acceptance of the losses he has. Why did my son get sick? I will never accept that." We replied, "That your son was affected by illness was beyond your control and therefore not something you had the power to decide. The acceptance we are talking about does not mean taking responsibility for an illness that is not your fault. It is the acceptance of the very difficult feelings that accompany the losses you have as a result of this illness and giving yourself the opportunity to take these feelings seriously. We are talking about accepting that you have suffered a great loss and that you are responding to the losses you are experiencing."

> We believe that seeking acceptance of our loss
> does not mean that we should think that it was okay that we had this loss.
> Acceptance, however, is sooner daring to realize
> that the loss has happened outside of our control and daring to be in touch
>   with the grief it causes.

Lack of acceptance can suppress many of our powers over time. As has been described in Chapters 3, 4, and 5, the physical, emotional, and cognitive responses can be very intense immediately after the loss, but when it is no longer necessary to avoid the initial anxiety, a clarity and strange calmness can emerge by daring to look at reality and life. This is the essence of the paradoxical power of acceptance. In these moments, it can feel as if our senses, emotions, and mind are aligned and focused, providing us with clarity and a paradoxical peace in the pain.

The IPM describes how we are usually not aware that not only does loss cause deficiency and absence, but we also develop a type of superpowers in the wake of a loss. It occurs when we understand that the vulnerability we experience can develop into humility and sensitivity that helps us to be in closer touch with ourselves and life, endure our pain, and even acknowledge the pain of others. It happens when the intense emotional fluctuations of grief help us develop emotional regulation and flexibility; when the inner cognitive struggles of grief can result in increased reflection, new insight and bodily awareness; when the void left by loss can lead us toward a deeper sense of connectedness with ourselves and others; and when the meaninglessness and disbelief push us to find a deeper meaning, hope, and trust.

In a novel, a loss is often the point in the story where the main character goes from living a normal everyday life to something decisive happening. Now, the main character must go on a quest, which forces the person to enter a completely new world and seek a new goal. This new world is not always literal but often mostly inside ourselves and definitely outside our comfort zone. Think of Cinderella losing her mother, Harry Potter losing his parents, Alice in Wonderland falling down the rabbit hole, poor Charlie winning the golden ticket to enter the chocolate factory, and many other stories. Various losses give them an initial push to get their story going. Along the way, there are various turning points or defining moments in which something happens that causes a shift or change in the direction they are going. The turning point moves their narrative forward. The turning point can be obstacles that the main character has to overcome, a sacrifice in which the person has to give up something important or something of himself in order to achieve a goal or save someone; an opportunity like a lottery ticket or new friends; a choice in which the person must actively decide something to increase the chances of success; a chance where the person can do something different and hope it pays off; a decisive decision in which the person finds out something new that forces new decisions, and last but not least, a realization in which the person learns something new and changes his values or his outlook on life.

Turning points seem to work best in the great narratives when they have been earned, which means that they are usually achieved after hard work, sacrifice, and character-building courage and determination. If the story is to really have meaning, then the journey should preferably be both physical and metaphorical. In the great stories, it is clear that a great loss comes with a series of challenges, suffering, choices, decisions, opportunities, and realizations. The question is whether we can see ourselves in the great narrative and recognize the turning points. At each turning point, the person usually learns something about themselves, and by the end of the great narratives, the person is very different from the character at the initial defining moment. The stories point out that once the turning point has happened, the person can never go back to being the same person. The story can only move forward from there. Where is the main character going?

The paradox of grief's transformative potential is
that personal strength grows out of vulnerability,
that it is through the emotional chaos in grief that we achieve greater flexibility,
that it is the isolation of loss that spurs us to seek more connectedness,
and that it is on the basis of our existential doubts that we develop
a deeper faith, more meaning, or a deeper set of values.

The pitfalls are that we have the possibility of denying our vulnerability and not seeing the shared characteristics with the rest of humanity, which makes it difficult to seek connectedness. It may also be that we do not find a way to express the grief in a meaningful way because we do not recognize the extent of the loss, or we attach certain meaning to different events so that everything becomes spiritualized. Or that we either avoid our feelings or drown in them and make grief a new life task because we do not find the balance between holding on and letting go. Last but not least, that we are not open to look for meaning after the loss, and therefore not open to new goals in life, or to how the sensation of resonance and vitality can help us.

Table 8.1 IPM points of orientation

Dimension	Existential tension	Transformative potential	Points of orientation	Central questions
Physical	Accepting death – Embracing life	From vulnerability personal strength can grow. *Pitfall:* Denying vulnerability Lack of stabilization of bodily grief Hastened death	Seeking connection with oneself Seek to stabilize bodily reaction Accepting death Balancing life and death. Embracing your own vulnerability	How can I stabilize my body? How can I live with the reality of the loss? How will I get acquainted with loss and death?
Emotional	Being – Taking responsibility	From emotional chaos, a flexible approach to the emotions can be achieved. *Pitfall:* Avoiding emotions Drowning in emotions Turning grief into a new life task	Being patient with yourself and others Seeking self-care Exploring ways to regulate emotional responses Being brave and taking responsibility for working with feelings of grief	How can I practice self-care? How/when do I connect to my grief? How can I honor my grief?
Cognitive	Reflective awareness – Bodily awareness	From the awareness of the loss, a new understanding of life can arise. *Pitfall:* Magical thinking ("what if" thoughts) Profit seeking Not expressing grief meaningfully	Honesty Seeking acceptance of adversity Getting to know your grief Daring to change assumptions about life Allowing meaning construction	What is my grief about? How can I get acquainted with my grief? How can I grieve this loss meaningfully?

Social Aloneness - Connectedness	From the loss of a relationship, deeper relationships can grow *Pitfall:* Lack of connection to others and recognition of shared vulnerability Social escape; not accepting aloneness. Either holding on or letting go (completely)	Seeking connectedness Seeing the existential vulnerability in all of us Looking for the feeling of belonging and sharing Balancing holding on and letting go Using longing as a guideline for new goals	How can I continue the bond? How can I let go of/change the bond? How can I reach out to others and connect?
Spiritual Meaning - Meaninglessness	From spiritual doubt, deeper beliefs and values can be formed. *Pitfall:* Spiritualize everything or give meaning to everything Nihilism Not being open to new goals in life, not reviving resonance/vitality	Seeking engagement in existential issues Reflecting on existential meaning, values, sense of purpose Using existential values as a compass Openness to pursue new goals Rediscovering your own capacity for creativity and growth	How is this loss changing my understanding of life? How can I find meaning again? What are my revised goals in life?

Loss and grief can be understood as a hurricane inside us that causes chaos, and we constantly work to find balance living the existential paradoxes that have become clear to us. If not answered, these existential openings will close themselves again, as will the invitation to reflect on the tensions to find a better balance in life. Then, there is the risk that our own losses and grief leave us without us developing this understanding or the sensitivity to the loss and pain of others; and then, there is the risk that we contribute to denying the losses of others, avoid taking our shared human vulnerabilities serious, or we may even continue without a clear sense of meaning in life. Instead, we spend our time feeling like victims of life fighting over whose loss is the worst. Now, there is a risk that we make our loss a new theme in our lives, or we stop looking for how our goals in life can be developed in a dynamic process with life itself.

Imbalances in grief

Our autobiographical history, experiences, and personal resources undeniably play a role in how we approach our loss, just as the reaction to our loss is defined by what we lost, what it meant to us, and how we lost it. All of these aspects make up our personal place in our grief. Seen through the lens of the IPM, the ultimate questions and existential tensions opened up by the particular loss we have suffered will also play a significant role. The IPM aims to explain how we will all have different ways of grieving, different challenges with the loss, different existential tensions to wrestle with, and even different aspects to learn from it. In fact, the IPM points out that our struggles with loss also are determined by our personal existential struggles and the parts of our personality that might existentially benefit from maturing. There is always a personal positioning in our imbalances in the existential tensions. Loss and grief open up these existential tensions for us, some of which are also old familiar internal struggles that can now feel more polarized and intense than ever.

> Loss reveals existential imbalances in our life
> and urges us to revisit these imbalances.
> Grief invites us to confront them
> and find a better balance in life.

This can pertain to the balance between loneliness and connectedness. If we feel alone in life and struggle with the feeling of aloneness, then this imbalance will be reinforced in grief. Or if we have placed our connectedness very narrowly in one person or job, then we are at higher risk of losing what we were connected to. It may also be that we struggle with strong emotions that overwhelm us, and the understanding of freedom or choice in grief is absent, because we experience grief as if it places demands that cannot be honored (see also Chapter 4). Or we struggle to even understand our loss and therefore continue to talk about it to integrate it into our thinking, as was described in Chapter 5 of *Grief as a Learning Process* by Mary-Frances O'Connor (O'Connor, 2022). However, all these examples are not only about imbalances within the person but also about a lack of understanding and knowledge in society. Our imbalances in grief can also be seen in the light of our struggles with the implicit grieving rules and cultural rituals or expectations of others in society. This sometimes leaves little room for, for example, expressing relief when we have lost a close person, or showing anger when we have lost a job or an expectation in life, or showing guilt when the loss was also partially self-inflicted. Not to mention that there can be an overall lack of understanding and recognition of our loss and grief in the process of unrecognized loss, which is described by Kenneth Doka in Chapter 6 (Doka, 1989, 2023). However natural these feelings or expressions of grief may be in the wake of loss, there is a tendency toward a lack of a comprehensive understanding of grief that means that the expressions are not tolerated or recognized as falling within acceptable norms. This can result in us withdrawing from social contact when we are in grief, or we feel ashamed and engage in self-criticism when we do not experience the space, security, and support for our grief reaction.

Grief disorder

One of the types of imbalances that has received a lot of attention is the imbalance expressed in the diagnosis of prolonged grief disorder (PGD). Much research on loss and grief has looked at the agony of loss and the risk of psychopathology. Prolonged grief disorder has been described as "getting stuck" in the grieving process and struggling with peritraumatic reactions that are not recognized or stabilized, being emotionally overwhelmed by grief, or cognitively suffering from circular ruminations that do not create more balance in mind, emotions, or behavior (Killikelly & Maercker, 2018). The diagnostic criteria include that the imbalance is so severe and the duration so long that there is a clinically significant functional impairment due to the imbalance in the grief.

Although the IPM is not a model of complications in grief, the IPM describes exactly that we can get stuck in each of the dimensions of loss and grief if the tensions are not balanced.

According to the IPM, complications can be due to a lack of balance in the various dimensions:

- The physical dimension: that the body is not stabilized. That we do not understand that loss happens to everyone.
- The emotional dimension: that emotions are not regulated.
- The cognitive dimension: that magical thinking and lack of acceptance or recognition of the loss continue unchanged. That we do not get to know our grief.

- The social dimension: that we do not find new connectedness but live with the feeling of loneliness. That we do not find a balance in holding on and letting go.
- The spiritual dimension: that we do not find new meaning or hope so that faith in life is restored.

These imbalances will mean that we do not find a balance in life's big questions and therefore cannot get in contact with our grief in an authentic way. The IPM can be used to increase our understanding of loss and grief as comprehensive experiences, and so are the processes we enter into and the existential tensions in them. Here, the IPM addresses a number of points that can be helpful in navigating our grief reactions and some questions that will be able to support the bereaved.

Text box 8.2   Questions that can help prevent imbalances in grief

- What is your grief about?
- How can you express it meaningfully and honor the loss?
- How can you find a balance in grief so that you can live with your loss?
- How can you seek connectedness now?
- How can you regain faith in life and find resonance and meaning in life?

Facilitating the integrative understanding of grief

The purpose of facilitating grief
is not to escape the grief
or get on the other side of it.
Rather, it is to restore
connectedness with oneself and with grief.
It is when we can be in contact with our grief
that we can find a way to live with it.

When providing support to a grieving person, acting like a mechanic trying to carry out a repair and focusing on mechanisms as pathology, complications, symptom relief, or diagnosis is unlikely to succeed. When providing support to a grieving person, acting like a gardener who understands loss and grief as natural existential experiences is more likely to succeed because the focus is on feeding the unique

Cognitive
What is my grief about?
How can I get acquainted
with my grief?
How can I grieve this loss
meaningfully?

Social
How can I continue the bond?
How can I let go of/change the bond?
How can I reach out to others and
connect?

Reflective - embodied awareness

Aloneness - Connectedness

Integrative Process Model

Being - Responsibility

Meaning - Meaninglessness

Spiritual
How is this loss changing my
understanding of life?
How can I find meaning again?
What are my revised goals in life?

Emotional
How can I practice self-care?
How/when do I connect to my
grief?
How can I honor my grief?

Embracing life - accepting death

Physical
How can I stabilize my body?
How can I live with the
reality of the loss?
How will I get acquainted
with loss and death?

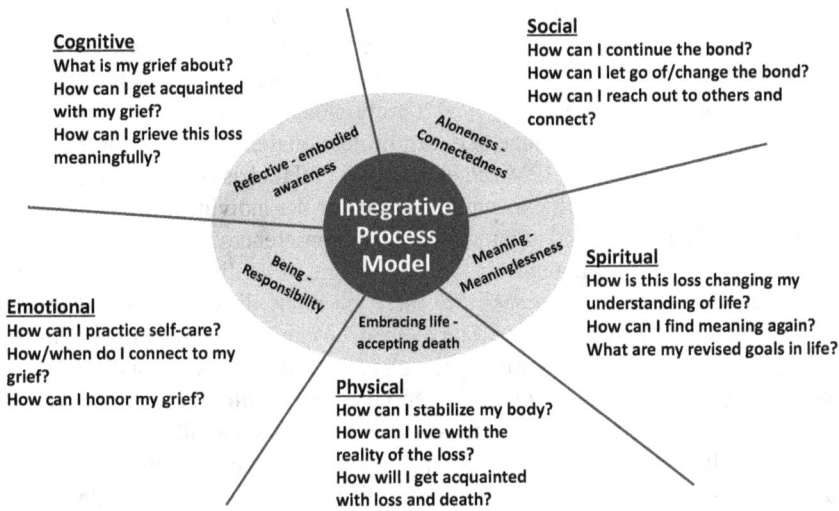

Figure 8.2 IPM facilitating questions from Table 8.1 depicted in a model with five segments, bringing together all questions as they are related to the existential tensions.

plant to help it grow. The IPM underlines that entering into an existential dialogue facilitates grief while patiently searching for contact with the grief in order to honor what has been lost and give the grief a meaningful expression.

The IPM proposes a series of central questions that point in the direction of living the questions in loss and grief that are exposed to us if we are open to seeing them. These questions are based on the transformative potentials described in Chapters 3 through 7. The idea is that the questions can help to find a balance in the existential tensions that open into the dimensions when we "do" our grief. Clearly, there are many existential points of reference and questions in life, and the IPM introduces but a few research-based questions, although there are many other possible questions. The proposed facilitating questions become apparent when we pay attention and ask existential questions to increase our awareness of the anxieties and tensions.

The purpose of the approach in the IPM is to create an interprofessional framework for all disciplines to increase knowledge and awareness of the phenomenon of grief. The idea is that the IPM can be useful for all professionals from all professional groups. Although professionals work from different frames of reference that are used to interpret the process taking place, here, the basis for the IPM is that our primary frame of reference is the interpretive framework that uses our profession as a point of departure, for example, that the psychologist is trained to look for pathologies or the chaplain works from an understanding of a certain religious tradition or outlook on life. In the IPM, the idea is that each professional group is aware of all dimensions of grief, even if we all work from a primary interpretive framework. If we can combine our primary frame of reference with a secondary frame of reference from another discipline or even an awareness of the integrated process, it opens up the possibility of a wider range of understandings that can better support the person in grief (Mooren, 1989). If working in an interdisciplinary or interprofessional context, as many health professionals do, this distinction can be useful in maintaining the balance between professional expertise and integration. Taking this into account, the IPM can even be a useful tool as competence development around loss, grief, and existential aspects for the individual professional, in multiprofessional teams, and at interdisciplinary conferences.

The IPM is primarily about how we can honor and facilitate the grieving process by encouraging an awareness that there are many different types of loss in life that we may need support for. The expressions and processes of grief unfold in the physical, emotional, cognitive, social, and spiritual-existential dimensions. Loss also invites the great ultimate existential concerns into our lives and asks us to balance fundamental existential tensions as we grieve. Facilitating grief therefore means listening to the body, paying attention to the regulation of senses, emotions, and thoughts, and being open to discovering new connectedness and vitality. In grief facilitation, this moment (here-and-now), the body, and the nervous system are of great help and can help guide us as concrete anchors in grief.

> When providing care and support to people with loss and grief,
> it is important to have the courage
> to invite the existential tensions into the room
> even if you do not have the answers.

Here, it is more important to be willing to use one's own authenticity to reflect on the balance and point to key questions because it can help the process forward. Over time, it can also mean that you dare to reflect on the transformative potential of the experience of loss and grief. The IPM offers a framework that can be used to provide professional support, advice, and therapy but also support in groups and communities and even self-care.

The IPM has been developed as a framework to integrate different understandings and models of loss and grief to work interdisciplinarily in supporting people with loss and grief. The IPM is a model that offers an integrated understanding of loss and grief, a model for working existentially with loss and grief, a mirror for our own losses and grief, and also a model that can be used to increase professionals' skills in the field of loss and grief, because it points to how to open up a multidimensional conversation about loss and grief.

> Working with the IPM means having the courage to face the grief
> and engage in it with the intention of alleviating the suffering
> but not necessarily with the idea that the grief will end.

This requires knowledge of what grief is and that we can develop skills and competencies to work with another person's grief and pain. It also requires the awareness that every human being experiences loss and suffering and to have a realization that loss and grief open us to the ultimate concerns of life and to the great existential paradoxes.

> The overall idea of the IPM is to have the capacity to face the other person's grief with compassion and to have inner space to face the pain and at the same time know the difference between wanting to help navigate the grief and wanting to correct the suffering.

The IPM can be used as a model to talk about and live the issues of our own loss and grief and be able to help others when they are confronted with loss and grief.

> Of course, it would be easier if the IPM, like previous models,
> could provide the answers to where the mourner should go,
> how grief ends, what the goals are in a grieving process, etc.
> The problem, however, is that this is not how loss and grief work in us.

Previous models have created misunderstandings about grief and narrow frameworks about how to provide bereavement care. Instead, the IPM points to a number of research-based orientation points, which aim to create an interprofessional framework for all professional groups and to increase awareness of the phenomena of grief and understand how to support the other person in living with and expressing their grief meaningfully. The IPM suggests that one way to do this is for us to recognize that loss and grief not only bring pain but also open up a space for existential tension that invites us into the awareness of this space's potential to create resonance, transcendence, and transformation. Still, there is no guarantee that the IPM is helpful, just as there is no guarantee that we find meaning, friendship, or love in life.

Loss and grief are what can be called spontaneous life utterances. They cannot be solved, there are no shortcuts, no professional tricks, no golden questions that do all the work for us, no secret answers we can steer by, and no quick fixes to employ. Suffering a loss does not act as a pit stop in a race. Rather, it works like the work of a farmer who grows delicate vegetables. We need patience, knowledge, maybe a little luck, but especially a good sense of the losses we are working with.

> We can help others with their grief by living the questions ourselves
> and being open to them in a conversation
> when we turn to the grief.

To live the questions in loss and grief

This book opened with telling an ancient Chinese parable. It invited us to understand the ambiguity of loss and pointed to the paradox that when there is loss, there will also be a gain, even if we do not see it at first. Sometimes, the payoff may be gaining a broader understanding of good and bad events in life and letting go of preconceived notions. At other times, loss forces us to live with the big questions in life. Then, the loss can shift our entire understanding of meaning in life, and we experience an existential transformation of our values and personal immersion in the meaning of life. Therefore, this book ends with a new version of the parable, which is our own version and reflects the main points of the book.

Once upon a time, there was a righteous man who lived near the border. One day, one of his horses broke loose and ran into barbarian territory. All his neighbors felt sorry for him, but his father said, "It is true, we 'lost' a horse. That is how life is sometimes. We were happy with the horse, but the horse did not belong to us, only to himself. Let us keep our minds open and see what the real significance of this event will be in the bigger picture of our lives." After a few months, the horse returned, bringing with him a group of good barbarian horses. Everyone congratulated the man, but his father said, "It is good to be blessed with wealth, but let us keep our minds open and take in that all that we have can be both a source of joy and a source of sorrow. There is no gain without loss." When the man's son was out riding one of the horses, he fell off and broke a leg. All the neighbors felt sorry for him, but the father said, "Breaking a leg is a painful but normal event in life. Let us keep our minds open and take loving care of our vulnerability, because sometimes, our vulnerability is our strength." A year later, the barbarians invaded the country, and all men had to join the army to defend the country. The son who had broken his leg was exempted and allowed to stay at home. In the battle that followed, nine out of ten frontiersmen were killed, but both father and son survived. In the process of facing the enormous losses the war had inflicted on them, father and son grew increasingly grateful and humble, embracing life more fully than they ever had before.

The IPM opens a space for the awareness that we live the existential questions that loss initiates and that we can have a conversation about the big questions in life. It helps developing an attitude for the meeting with the bereaved. It supports meeting the other in a space where there is an understanding of the many dimensions of loss and grief and which is open to the existential dimension in the process. The quality of the meeting is largely determined by the facilitator's personal training and ability to be a space with resonance for the bereaved's experiences, feelings, and thoughts. Next to this, of course, there are many other factors that play a role in the quality of the meeting, such as context, timing, situation, nonverbal, and bodily signals, etc. There-fore, it is impossible to formulate central questions, which are always the best way to open a conversation. Nevertheless, a large number of questions for existential reflec-tion are presented throughout the book. Some key questions in each dimension of the IPM are also presented here, which can be useful for orientation and to get an idea of how conversations in the five dimensions can develop. It is important to realize that the best way to ask questions is to be present with your presence and authenticity. In that sense, the IPM is not only intended to facilitate the process of development toward the authenticity of the mourner; an important prerequisite is also the facilita-tor's authenticity and own awareness of existential tensions and life's big questions.

The IPM is about how we can learn to live with all our losses and with grief as a natural part of life, without there being specific answers and solutions. With this approach, the goal is to gain a more comprehensive understanding of what role loss and grief play in a life course and how they are at the same time an experience that can help us into a deeper understanding of life and to becoming more authentic. In existential themes, there are no specific coping strategies that will always be able to ease our existential concerns. The strength of an existential tension is that we must constantly balance it without ever arriving at a final position or point of view. Although the tensions underpin all grieving processes, they cannot be resolved or cured, but we can make choices and try to be brave enough to reflect on them so they can help us balance our existence. In doing so, we may discover that grief, despite the despair and suffering, can also become an opening to connection with ourselves and a deeper understanding of life.

Central points in Chapter 8

- The idea of the IPM is not that we will experience more happiness as a result of daring to deal with our grief. But if we dare to feel our grief, developing more existential awareness can enable us to experience more intense satisfaction and inner peace, because we can use our understand-ing of existential meaning as a compass.
- Loss aversion means that we tend to value losses as much more powerful than what we can gain from the loss. It is likely that our fear of death and loss stand in the way of living freely.
- Nevertheless, loss and grief can also result in positive change that is described as posttraumatic growth.
- Personal growth in grief is often expressed as learning about the person them-selves, their character and personal strengths, as increased relational knowl-edge, or as existential learning about life, death, loneliness, or meaning.
- The IPM differs significantly from previous models of grief, since it does not point to a specific goal for the grieving process but rather to the para-dox that loss can turn into growth if we are open to living the questions of our existence.

- The paradoxical theory of change explains that the moment we accept the loss, we can begin to look at it and thus enter into a quest to live with it.
- Loss reveals existential imbalances in life and urges us to revisit our personal imbalances. Grief invites us to confront them and find a better balance in life.
- The purpose of facilitating grief is not to escape the grief or get on the other side of it. Rather, it is to restore the griever's connectedness with oneself and with grief. It is in contact with our grief that we can find a way to live with it.
- The IPM can be used in an interprofessional framework that helps to cooperate in facilitating grief care and therapy, integrating knowledge from different disciplines for the benefit of the griever and family system.

Postlude: Ann's balance in loss and grief

As for the story of Ann: perhaps she was searching the top of the tree for something that could only be found in her roots, as the Persian poet Rumi would have said (Rumi, Goodreads).

Ann's loss and grief put her in touch with her past. It was very painful to feel isolated from the rest of humanity after all she had achieved in life, and although she was still proud of her achievements, she no longer felt the need to work until she was depleted from exhaustion to reduce feelings of loneliness and desolation. It had occurred to her how the feeling of deep inner isolation had started in childhood, and although it was not her fault, she felt ashamed of it. It helped her see that it was a natural part of her life story. This was the great challenge she faced after her recent losses: to accept the deep sense of emptiness and isolation while being more aware of the great losses in her life and the mechanisms within herself that prevented deep connectedness with other people for fear of not being found worthy of love and being rejected. Ann slowly began to realize that every life story has its losses, failures, and unfulfilled dreams. It gave her both a deeper sense of herself and also an understanding of being part of a vulnerable life that she shared with others. It made her rethink her identity and her goals in life. Ann gradually realized that she would have to accept the deep wounds of her early youth and take responsibility for the choices she had made in life while also integrating new ways of connecting with people. She worked to find resonance in the world through aspects other than romantic relationships, such as enjoying yoga classes to feel in touch with her body, joining a hiking group to spend her Sundays in nature, and volunteering for a small local art gallery for local artists. In this way, she gained a stronger sense of community, developed new meaningful goals in life, and found small moments of connectedness with people who shared her appreciation of art and nature. Ann was especially grateful for being able to create a new connectedness with herself through the wake-up call her losses had given her.

Ann slowly gained a greater understanding of her losses in life and how they had affected her: not only losing her mother at a young age but also her father's alcohol problem and the feeling of not being wanted in life. The loss of a boyfriend who she was considering spending old age with confronted her with never having experienced unconditional love from anyone. Although it helped her develop a sense of inner strength and purpose, she had not always been in touch with her own senses and needs, because this was not part of her upbringing. She had attached herself to life in a way that she would later characterize as having a need for achievement to feel she had a right to take up space in the world. As her mind and body began to change through menopause, she initially felt vulnerable and weak, but it also forced her to get in touch with her own body and basic needs for sleep, rest, and calm. This was a major turning point for Ann, to find a new connectedness with her body and, through listening to the body's signals, also experience a deeper connectedness between body and mind. In some ways, this new unity between body and mind gave her a new perspective on life and on what was important.

Through more self-care and by occasionally taking time off from work, Ann gradually got more in touch with the nuances of her feelings and her old losses in life. It felt like accessing a deeper part of herself and no longer feeling like she had to overcome or fight her own past. Looking at these decisive losses in her life gave her the insight and clarity to also get in touch with the emptiness and loneliness she had felt when making decisions not to marry, not to have children, and to live her life in solitude.

It was a real eye-opener for her to learn that she had always longed to belong somewhere or to feel wanted and accepted. She accepted her choices over her lifetime and understood that they had given her so much in return. However, she realized that she had not been open to the vulnerability and unpredictability of working closely with others. By ensuring that she was always in charge in her working relationships, she had not been truly confronted with other people's ideas and thereby missed out on inspiring collaborations and deeper working relationships. The same had played out in her romantic relationships, where in retrospect, she may have sought more control than change. From her new vantage point, it was easier to see that the deep longing for connectedness would have required more trust in the men she had dated and required her to share the vulnerability she would feel. This gave her a feeling of sadness and loneliness when the independence that used to make her feel strong now seemed like a fence against being connected. The new connectedness she found with her friends through the honest sharing of her vulnerability and sadness gradually gave way to a deeper resonance in her friendships. Volunteering at the local art gallery evoked a sense of inspiration and transcendence because she could put her business skills to work in a more creative and fun way.

References

Andersen, H. C. (2014). *The complete fairy tales*. Printers Row Publishing Group. (Original work published 1847)

Aoun, S. M., Breen, L. J., O'Connor, M., Rumbold, B., & Nordstrom, C. (2012). A public health approach to bereavement support services in palliative care. *Australian and New Zealand Journal of Public Health, 36*(1), 14–16.

Aoun, S. M., Richmond, R., Gunton, K., Noonan, K., Abel, J., & Rumbold, B. (2022). The compassionate communities connectors model for end-of-life care: Implementation and evaluation. *Palliative Care and Social Practice, 16*, 1–18.

Averill, J. R., & Nunley, E. P. (1988). Grief as an emotion and as a disease: A social-constructionist perspective. *Journal of Social Issues, 44*, 79–95.

Balboni, T. A., Fitchett, G., Handzo, G., Johnson, K. S., Koenig, H. G., Pargament, K. I., Puchalski, C. M., Sinclair, S., Taylor, E. J., & Steinhauser, K. E. (2017). State of the science of spirituality and palliative care research part II: Screening, assessment, and interventions. *Journal of Pain and Symptom Management, 54*(3), 441–453.

Bayard, F. (1999). *L'art du bien mourir au XVe siècle*. Presses de l'université Paris-Sorbonne.

Beisser, A. (1970). The paradoxical theory of change. In J. Fagan & I. L. Shepherd (Eds.), *Gestalt therapy now: Theory, techniques, applications*. Harper & Row.

Bernstein, L. (1976). *The unanswered question: Six talks at Harvard*. Harvard University Press.

Boelen, P. A. (2015). Peritraumatic distress and dissociation in prolonged grief and posttraumatic stress following violent and unexpected deaths. *Journal of Trauma & Dissociation, 16*(5), 541–550.

Boelen, P. A., & Lenferink, L. I. (2020). Symptoms of prolonged grief, posttraumatic stress, and depression in recently bereaved people: Symptom profiles, predictive value, and cognitive behavioural correlates. *Social Psychiatry and Psychiatric Epidemiology, 55*, 765–777.

Bonanno, G. A., & Burton, C. L. (2013). Regulatory flexibility: An individual differences perspective on coping and emotion regulation. *Perspectives on Psychological Science, 8*(6), 591–612.

Bonanno, G. A., Westphal, M., & Mancini, A. D. (2011). Resilience to loss and potential trauma. *Annual Review of Clinical Psychology, 7*, 511–535.

Bowlby, J. (1980). *Attachment and loss*. Hogarth.

Brant, J. (2017). Holistic total pain management in palliative care: Cultural and global considerations. *Palliative Medicine and Hospice Care, 1*, S32–S38.

Brennan, F., & Dash, M. (2009). The year of magical thinking: Joan Didion and the dialectic of grief. *Bereavement Care, 28*(2), 31–36.

Breuer, J., & Freud, S. (1895). Studies on hysteria. In *Standard edition* (Vol. 2). Vintage, The Hogarth Press.

Bukowski, C. (2002). No help for that. In *You get so alone at times that it just makes sense.* Ecco. (Original work published 1986)

Byron, L. G. G. (2021). *Childe Harold's pilgrimage.* Graphic Arts Books. (Original work published 1812–1818)

Camus, A. (1989). *The stranger.* Vintage. (Original work published 1942)

Cholbi, M. (2022). *Grief: A philosophical guide.* Princeton University Press.

Clark, D. (1999). "Total pain", disciplinary power and the body in the work of Cicely Saunders, 1958–1967. *Social Science & Medicine, 49*(6), 727–736.

Coelho, P. (2014). *The alchemist.* Harper One. (Original work published 1988)

Cooper, M. (2003). *Existential therapies* (2nd ed.). Sage Publications Ltd.

Craig, E. (2008). A brief overview of existential depth psychotherapy. *The Humanistic Psychologist, 36*(3–4), 211–226.

de La Rochefoucauld, F. (2008). *Collected Maxims and other reflections.* Oxford University Press. (Original work published 1665)

de Spinoza, B. (1955). *Ethics.* Dover. (Original work published 1677)

Didion, J. (2005). *The year of magical thinking.* Knopf.

Dilthey, W. (1883). *Einleitung in die Geisteswissenschaften: Versuch einer Grundlegung für das Studium der Gesellschaft und der Geschichte* (Bd. 1). Duncker & Humblot.

Dixon, T. (2012). "Emotion": The history of a keyword in crisis. *Emotion Review, 4*(4), 338–344.

Doka, K. J. (1989). *Disenfranchised grief: Recognizing hidden sorrow.* Jossey-Bass.

Doka, K. J. (2023). Bereavement: A sociological perspective. In E. M. Steffen, E. Milman, & R. A. Neimeyer (Eds.), *The handbook of grief therapies.* Sage Publications Ltd.

Durant, W. (1926). *The story of philosophy.* Simon & Schuster.

Einstein, A. (2000). *The expanded quotable Einstein* (A. Calaprice, Ed.). Princeton University Press.

Epictetus. (135/1983). *The handbook (Enchiridion).* Hackett Publishing Company.

Fiore, J. (2021). A systematic review of the dual process model of coping with bereavement (1999–2016). *OMEGA-Journal of Death and Dying, 84*(2), 414–458.

Frankl, V. E. (1967). *Psychotherapy and existentialism.* Washington Square Press.

Frankl, V. E. (2006). *Man's search for meaning.* Beacon Press. (Original work published 1946)

Freud, S. (1929). Letter from Sigmund Freud to Ludwig Binswanger, April 11, 1929. *Letters of Sigmund Freud 1873–1939, 51,* 386.

Freud, S. (1957). Mourning and melancholia (J. Strachey, Trans.). In J. Strachey (Ed.), *The standard edition of the complete psychological works of Sigmund Freud* (Vol. 14). Hogarth Press, Institute of Psychoanalysis. (Original work published 1917)

Frost, R. (1969). Desert places. In *The poetry of Robert Frost.* Holt, Rinehart & Winston. (Original work published 1933)

Gibran, K. (2019). *The prophet.* Penguin Classics. (Original work published 1923)

Gijsberts, M.-J. H., Liefbroer, A. I., Otten, R., & Olsman, E. (2019). Spiritual care in palliative care: A systematic review of the recent European literature. *Medical Sciences, 7*(2), 25.

Girard-Augry, P. (1986). *Ars moriendi (1492) ou L'art de bien mourir.* Dervy.

Granek, L. (2010). Grief as pathology: The evolution of grief theory in psychology from Freud to the present. *History of Psychology, 13*(1), 46–73.

Greene, J. (2012). *The fault in our stars.* Penguin Books.

Gross, J. J. (2014). Emotion regulation: Conceptual and empirical foundations. In J. J. Gross (Ed.), *Handbook of emotion regulation.* Guilford Press.

Guldin, M.-B. (2018). *Sorgterapi: Evidens og metoder i praksis.* Akademisk Forlag.

Guldin, M.-B. (2019). *Tab og sorg: En gundbog for professionelle* (2nd ed.). Hans Reitzels Forlag.

Guldin, M.-B., Ina Siegismund Kjaersgaard, M., Fenger-Grøn, M., Thorlund Parner, E., Li, J., Prior, A., & Vestergaard, M. (2017). Risk of suicide, deliberate self-harm and psychiatric illness after the loss of a close relative: A nationwide cohort study. *World Psychiatry*, *16*(2), 193–199.

Guldin, M.-B., & Leget, C. (2023). The integrated process model of loss and grief: An interprofessional understanding. *Death Studies*, *48*.

Gündel, H., O'Connor, M. F., Littrell, L., Fort, C., & Lane, R. D. (2003). Functional neuroanatomy of grief: An FMRI study. *American Journal of Psychiatry*, *160*(11), 1946–1953.

Hansen, K. L., Guldin, M.-B., & Fosgerau, C. F. (2023). Grief participation rights and the social support hierarchy: Exploring the communicative role of the bereaved in a social support interaction. *Death Studies*, 1–13.

Haufe, M., Leget, C., & Glasner, T., Teunissen, S., & Potma, M. (2022). Spiritual conversation model for patients and loved ones in palliative care: A validation study. *BMJ Supportive & Palliative Care*. Published Online First: 16 June 2022. doi: 10.1136/bmjspcare-2022-003569

Iglewicz, A., Shear, M. K., Reynolds, C. F., Simon, N., Lebowitz, B., & Zisook, S. (2020). Complicated grief therapy for clinicians: An evidence-based protocol for mental health practice. *Depression Anxiety*, *37*(1), 90–98.

Johannsen, M., Damholdt, M. F., Zachariae, R., Lundorff, M., Farver-Vestergaard, I., & O'Connor, M. (2019). Psychological interventions for grief in adults: A systematic review and meta-analysis of randomized controlled trials. *Journal of Affective Disorders*, *253*, 69–86.

Kahneman, D. (2012). *Thinking, fast and slow*. Penguin Books.

Kellehear, A. (2000). Spirituality and palliative care: A model of needs. *Palliative Medicine*, *14*(2), 149–155.

Kierkegaard, S. (1941). *Sickness until death*. Princeton University Press. (Original work published 1849)

Killikelly, C., & Maercker, A. (2018). Prolonged grief disorder for ICD-11: The primacy of clinical utility and international applicability. *European Journal of Psychotraumatology*, *8*(Suppl 6), 1476441.

Klass, D. (2006). Continuing conversation about continuing bonds. *Death Studies*, *30*(9), 843–858.

Klass, D., Silverman, P. R., & Nickman, S. (2014). *Continuing bonds: New understandings of grief*. Taylor & Francis. (Original work published 1996)

Kübler-Ross, E. (1969). *On death and dying*. Macmillan.

Laager, J. (1996). *Ars moriendi. Die Kunst gut zu leben und zu sterben: Texte von Cicero bis Luther*. Manesse Verlag.

Lazarus, R., & Folkman, S. (1984). *Stress, appraisal, and coping*. Springer.

Leget, C. (1997). *Living with God: Thomas Aquinas on the relation between life on Earth and "life" after death*. Peeters.

Leget, C. (2007). Retrieving the Ars Moriendi tradition. *Medicine, Health Care and Philosophy*, *10*(3), 313–319.

Leget, C. (2008). *Van levenskunst tot stervenskunst: Over spiritualiteit in de palliatieve zorg*. Lannoo.

Leget, C. (2012). *Ruimte om te sterven: Een weg voor zieken, naasten en zorgverleners*. Lannoo.

Leget, C. (2017). *Art of living, art of dying: Spiritual care for a good death*. Jessica Kingsley Publishers.

Lindemann, E. (1944). Symptomatology and management of acute grief. *American Journal of Psychiatry*, *101*, 141–148.

Løgstrup, K. E. (1997). *The ethical demand*. University of Notre Dame Press. (Original work published 1956)

Lormans, T., de Graaf, E., van de Geer, J., van der Baan, F., Leget, C., & Teunissen, S. (2021). Toward a socio-spiritual approach? A mixed-methods systematic review on the social and spiritual needs of patients in the palliative phase of their illness. *Palliative Medicine, 35*(6), 1071–1098.

Lundorff, M., Holmgren, H., & Zachariae, R. (2017). Prevalence of prolonged grief disorder in adult bereavement: A systematic review and meta-analysis. *Journal of Affective Disorders, 212*, 138–149.

Malloy, M. (1988). Epitaph. In *My song for him who never sang to me*. Three Rivers Press.

Maslow, A. H. (1943). A theory of human motivation. *Psychological Review, 50*(4), 370–396.

Maslow, A. H. (2013). *Toward a psychology of being*. Simon and Schuster. (Original work published 1968)

May, R. (1953). *Man's search for himself*. WW Norton & Company.

McLean, D. (1972). Vincent. In *American pie*. United Artists Record.

Merleau-Ponty, M. (1945). *Phénoménologie de la perception*. Gallimard.

Mikulincer, M., & Shaver, P. R. (2022). An attachment perspective on loss and grief. *Current Opinion in Psychology, 45*, 101283.

Milman, E. J. (2022). Measuring the outcome of grief therapies. In E. M. Steffen, E. Milman, & R. A. Neimeyer (Eds.), *The handbook of grief therapies*. Sage Publications Ltd.

Milton, J. (2003). *Paradise lost*. Penguin Classics. (Original work published 1667)

Mooren, J. H. M. (1989). *Geestelijke verzorging en psychotherapie*. De Graaff.

Murakami, H. (2006). *Kafka on the shore*. Vintage. (Original work published 2002)

Naifeh, S., & Smith, G. W. (2011). *Van Gogh: The life*. Random House.

Neff, K. D. (2003). Self-compassion: An alternative conceptualization of a healthy attitude toward oneself. *Self and Identity, 2*(2), 85–101.

Neff, K. D. (2011). Self-compassion, self-esteem, and well-being. *Social and Personality Psychology Compass, 5*(1), 1–12.

Neimeyer, R. A. (2001). *Meaning reconstruction and the experience of loss*. American Psychological Association.

Neimeyer, R. A. (2011). Reconstructing meaning in bereavement. *Rivista di Psichiatria, 46*(5–6), 332–336.

Neimeyer, R. A. (2023). Grief therapy as a quest for meaning. In E. M. Steffen, E. Milman, & R. A. Neimeyer (Eds.), *The handbook of grief therapies*. Sage Publications Ltd.

Neimeyer, R. A., Breen, L. J., & Milman, E. (2023). The effectiveness of grief therapy: A meta-analytic perspective. In E. M. Steffen, E. Milman, & R. A. Neimeyer (Eds.), *The handbook of grief therapies*. Sage Publications Ltd.

Neimeyer, R. A., Pitcho-Prelorentzos, S., & Mahat-Shamir, M. (2021). "If only . . .": Counterfactual thinking in bereavement. *Death Studies, 45*(9), 692–701.

Newby, Z., & Toulson, R. E. (Eds.). (2019). *The materiality of mourning: Cross-disciplinary perspectives*. Routledge.

Niebuhr, R. (1932). *Serenity prayer*. Retrieved February 13, 2024, from https://en.wikipedia.org/wiki/Serenity_Prayer

Nielsen, M. K., Carlsen, A. H., Neergaard, M. A., Bidstrup, P. E., & Guldin, M. B. (2019). Looking beyond the mean in grief trajectories: A prospective, population-based cohort study. *Social Science & Medicine, 232*, 460–469.

Nolan, S., Saltmarsh, P., & Leget, C. (2011). Spiritual care in palliative care: Working towards an EAPC task force. *European Journal of Palliative Care, 18*(2), 86–89.

O'Connor, M.-F. (2019). Grief: A brief history of research on how body, mind, and brain adapt. *Psychosomatic Medicine, 81*(8), 731–738.

O'Connor, M.-F. (2022). *The grieving brain: The surprising science of how we learn from love and loss*. HarperOne.

Olshansky, S. (1962). Chronic sorrow: A response to having a mentally defective child. *Social Casework, 43*(4), 190–193.

Papa, A., Lancaster, N. G., & Kahler, J. (2014). Commonalities in grief responding across bereavement and non-bereavement losses. *Journal of Affective Disorder*, *161*, 136–143.

Park, C. L. (2013). The meaning making model: A framework for understanding meaning, spirituality, and stress-related growth in health psychology. *European Health Psychologist*, *15*(2), 40–47.

Parkes, C. M. (1972). *Bereavement: Studies of grief in adult life*. Tavistock.

Paul, J. (1963). Selina oder über die Unsterblichkeit der Seele. In N. Miller (Ed.), *Jean Paul: Sämtliche Werke. Abteilung I. Sechster Band*. Wissenschaftliche Buchgesellschaft. (Original work published 1847)

Pennebaker, J. W., Zech, E., & Rimé, B. (2001). Disclosing and sharing emotion: Psychological, social, and health consequences. In M. S. Stroebe, R. O. Hansson, W. Stroebe, & H. Schut (Eds.), *Handbook of bereavement research: Consequences, coping, and care*. American Psychological Association.

Pontoppidan, H. (2019). *Lucky per*. Ballantine Books. (Original work published 1904)

Prigerson, H. G., Horowitz, M. J., Jacobs, S. C., Parkes, C. M., Aslan, M., Goodkin, K., Raphael, B., Marwit, S. J., Wortman, C., Neimeyer, R. A., Bonanno, G., Block, S. D., Kissane, D., Boelen, P., Maercker, A., Litz, B. T., Johnson, J. G., First, M. B., & Maciejewski, P. K. (2009). Prolonged grief disorder: Psychometric validation of criteria proposed for DSM-V and ICD-11. *PLOS Medicine*, *6*(8), e1000121.

Prigerson, H. G., Kakarala, S., Gang, J., & Maciejewski, P. K. (2021). History and status of prolonged grief disorder as a psychiatric diagnosis. *Annual Revue of Clinical Psychology*, *17*, 109–126.

Ricoeur, P. (1992). *Oneself as another*. University of Chicago Press.

Rilke, R. M. (1949). *Letters of Rainer Maria Rilke, Vol. II: 1910–1926*. Vail-Ballou Press. (Original work published 1923)

Rilke, R. M. (2000). *Letters to a young poet*. New World Library. (Original work published 1929)

Rosa, H. (2020). *The uncontrollability of the world*. Polity Press.

Rowland, L., & Curry, O. S. (2019). A range of kindness activities boost happiness. *The Journal of Social Psychology*, *159*(3), 340–343.

Rumbold, B., Lowe, L., & Aoun, S. M. (2021). The evolving landscape: Funerals, cemeteries, memorialization, and bereavement support. *OMEGA-Journal of Death and Dying*, *84*(2), 596–616.

Rumi, J. Retrieved February 13, 2024, from www.goodreads.com

Sartre, J.-P. (2020). *Being and nothingness: An essay in phenomenological ontology*. Routledge. (Original work published 1943)

Schiller, F. (1984). Über das Erhabene. In *Sämtliche werke* (Bd. 5). Hanser Verlag. (Original work published 1796)

Schneider, J. M. (2000). *The overdiagnosis of depression: Recognizing grief and its transformative potential*. Seasons Press.

Shear, M. K. (2015). Clinical practice: Complicated grief. *New England Journal of Medicine*, *372*(2), 153–160.

Silverman, G. S., Baroiller, A., & Hemer, S. R. (2021). Culture and grief: Ethnographic perspectives on ritual, relationships and remembering. *Death Studies*, *45*(1), 1–8.

Soulages, P. (2014). Interview by Zoe Stillpass. *Interview Magazine*. Retrieved February 13, 2024, from www.interviewmagazine.com/art/pierre-soulages#_

Spinelli, E. (2005). *The interpreted world: An introduction to phenomenological psychology* (2nd ed.). Sage Publications Ltd.

Spinelli, E. (2015). *Practising existential therapy*. Sage Publications Ltd.

Steffen, E. M. (2023). Grief therapies for our times: A pluralistic proposition. In E. M. Steffen, E. Milman, & R. A. Neimeyer (Eds.), *The handbook of grief therapies*. Sage Publications Ltd.

Steinhauser, K. E., Fitchett, G., Handzo, G., Johnson, K. S., Koenig, H. G., Pargament, K. I., Puchalski, C. M., Sinclair, S., Taylor, E. J., & Balboni, T. A. (2017). State of the science of spirituality and palliative care research part I: Definitions, measurement, and outcomes. *Journal of Pain and Symptom Management, 54*(3), 428–440.

Stroebe, M. S., Hansson, R. O., Schut, H., & Stroebe, W. (2008). Bereavement research: Contemporary perspectives. In M. S. Stroebe, R. O. Hansson, W. Stroebe, & H. Schut (Eds.), *Handbook of bereavement research and practice: Advances in theory and intervention.* American Psychological Association.

Stroebe, M. S., Hansson, R. O., Stroebe, W., & Schut, H. (2001). Introduction: Concepts and issues in contemporary research on bereavement. In M. S. Stroebe, R. O. Hansson, & W. Stroebe (Eds.), *Handbook of bereavement research: Consequences, coping, and care.* American Psychological Association.

Stroebe, M. S., & Schut, H. (1999). The dual process model of coping with bereavement: Rationale and description. *Death Studies, 23*(3), 197–224.

Stroebe, M. S., & Schut, H. (2010). The dual process model of coping with bereavement: A decade on. *OMEGA-Journal of Death and Dying, 61*(4), 273–289.

Tagore, R. Retrieved February 27, 2024, from www.goodreads.com/quotes/9981823-the-one-who-plants-trees-knowing-that-he-will-never

Tedeschi, R. G., & Calhoun, L. G. (1996). The posttraumatic growth inventory: Measuring the positive legacy of trauma. *Journal of Traumatic Stress, 9*(3), 455–471.

Tedeschi, R. G., & Calhoun, L. G. (2008). Beyond the concept of recovery: Growth and the experience of loss. *Death Studies, 32*(1), 27–39.

Tonkin, L. (1996). Growing around grief—another way of looking at grief and recovery. *Bereavement Care, 15*(1), 10.

Twain, M. (1967). *Mark Twain's "which was the dream?" and other symbolic writings of the later years* (J. S. Tuckey, Ed.). University of California Press. (Original work published 1898)

van Deurzen, E. (2023). Existential therapy for grief. In E. M. Steffen, E. Milman, & R. A. Neimeyer (Eds.), *The handbook of grief therapies.* Sage Publications Ltd.

van Deurzen, E., & Adams, M. (2016). *Skills in existential counselling and psychotherapy* (2nd edition). Sage Publications Ltd.

van Heck, G. L., & de Ridder, D. T. D. (2008). Assessment of coping with loss: Dimensions and measurements. In M. S. Stroebe, R. O. Hansson, W. Stroebe, & H. Schut (Eds.), *Handbook of bereavement research and practice: Advances in theory and intervention* (pp. 449–470). American Psychological Association.

Varga, M. A. (2016). A quantitative study of graduate student grief experiences. *Illness, Crisis & Loss, 24*(3), 170–186.

Vedder, A., Boerner, K., & Stokes, J. E. (2022). A systematic review of loneliness in bereavement: Current research and future directions. *Current Opinion in Psychology, 43*, 48–64.

Vehling, S., & Kissane, D. W. (2018). Existential distress in cancer: Alleviating suffering from fundamental loss and change. *Psycho-Oncology, 27*(11), 2525–2530.

Vermandere, M., Bertheloot, K., Buyse, H., Deraeve, P., De Roover, S., Strubbe, L., Van Immerseel, I., Vermandere, S., Voss, M., & Aertgeerts, B. (2013). Implementation of the Ars Moriendi model in palliative home care: A pilot study. *Progress in Palliative Care, 21*(5), 278–285.

Vermandere, M., Warmenhoven, F., Van Severen, E., De Lepeleire, J., & Aertgeerts, B. (2015). The Ars Moriendi model for spiritual assessment: A mixed-methods evaluation. *Oncology Nursing Forum, 42*(4), 294–301.

von Goethe, J. W. (1988). *Faust: First part.* Bantam Classics. (Original work published 1808)

Wagner, B., Rosenberg, N., Hofmann, L., & Maass, U. (2020). Web-based bereavement care: A systematic review and meta-analysis. *Frontiers in Psychiatry, 11*, 525.

Walter, T. (1994). *The revival of death*. Routledge.

Walter, T. (2008). The new public mourning. In M. S. Stroebe, R. O. Hansson, W. Stroebe, & H. Schut (Eds.), *Handbook of bereavement research and practice: Advances in theory and intervention*. American Psychological Association.

Walter, T. (2020). *Death in the modern world*. Sage Publications Ltd.

Ware, B. (2019). *Top five regrets of the dying: A life transformed by the dearly departing*. Hay House UK Ltd. (Original work published 2011)

Wikipedia. Retrieved February 26, 2024, from https://en.wikipedia.org/wiki/The_old_man_lost_his_horse

Wikipedia. Retrieved February 27, 2024, from https://en.wikipedia.org/wiki/Orpheus_and_Eurydice

Wilde, O. (2015). *De Profundis and other prison writings*. Penguin Classics. (Original work published 1905)

Winnicott, D. W. (1958). The capacity to be alone. *The International Journal of Psychoanalysis, 39*, 416–420.

Worden, J. W. (1991). *Grief counseling and grief therapy: A handbook for the mental health practitioner*. Springer.

Yalom, I. D. (1980). *Existential psychotherapy*. Basic Books.

Yalom, I. D. (2016). *Creatures of a day*. Basic Books.

Index

For Product Safety Concerns and Information please contact our EU
representative GPSR@taylorandfrancis.com
Taylor & Francis Verlag GmbH, Kaufingerstraße 24, 80331 München, Germany